For those raised outside liturgical traditions, practices like reciting creeds, collective prayer, and feast days can often feel overwhelming or foreign. But with his new book, *Earth Filled with Heaven*, pastor and author Aaron Damiani invites readers to rediscover the patterns and rhythms that have sustained the church for generations. More than an explainer, this book unites us with saints around the world and throughout time, celebrating our shared Christian roots and the God who makes worship glorious by His presence.

HANNAH ANDERSON, author of *Turning of Days: Lessons from Nature, Season, and Spirit*

Ora et labora. These ancient words remind us that heaven is not far from earth; in fact, the truest truth is that a holy life is more seamless, a life where heaven and earth are woven together—if we have eyes to see. Drawing upon the liturgical richness of the church through the centuries, the longing of Aaron Damiani is to bring the contemporary reader into a fuller faith and hope and love. As comfortable in reflecting on the long lament of the Chicago Cubs as he is about the profound pedagogy of the Chronicles of Narnia, and much more, *Earth Filled with Heaven* is a catechism for our day, a pastoral call to know more completely what we believe and why we believe, but especially why it matters.

STEVEN GARBER, Senior Fellow for Vocation and the Common Good, and author of *The Seamless Life: A Tapestry of Love and Learning, Worship and Work*

Evangelicals need liturgy. The reason, explains Aaron Damiani, is that liturgy is all about Jesus. The Incarnation joins heaven and earth, a union that we experience nowhere more concretely than in the church's liturgy. Unapologetically sacramental, Damiani takes us back to the church's ancient practices, there to find renewed rest, peace, and hope. *Earth Filled with Heaven* is a stellar primer for evangelical Christians who long to deepen their lives with the real presence of Jesus Himself.

HANS BOERSMA, Professor of Ascetical Theology, Nashotah House Theological Seminary, and author of *Heavenly Participation: The Weaving of a Sacramental Tapestry*

Reading this book is like discovering a long-lost treasure chest in your own backyard. It is full of unfamiliar and exotic treasure and, lo and behold, it turns out those treasures belong to you! Many modern Protestant evangelicals are unaware that their own family worship tree includes a rich and vibrant liturgical and sacramental tradition whose purpose is to exalt and glorify Jesus Christ in every area of life. Aaron Damiani's book is perfectly suited to help us recover the riches we didn't know were ours, and to rediscover a way of church and a way of life that is infused with the presence of Jesus Christ.

MARCUS JOHNSON, Professor of Theology, Moody Bible Institute; associate rector at St. Mark's Church, Geneva, IL; author of *One with Christ: An Evangelical Theology of Salvation*

We live in a crazy and chaotic world where too many people have become burned out and disenchanted with the church. Rather than giving up on the faith, Aaron Damiani has written a book that introduces readers to timeless practices of the church for challenging times. Read it and you will find your faith refreshed and renewed in the ancient rhythms of grace.

WINFIELD BEVINS, author of *Liturgical Mission* and *Ever Ancient, Ever New*

At a time when the evangelical movement is splintered and tribal, this book calls us back the slow, patient rhythms that have marked the historic Christian church. We've been taught that rituals without relationships can be dead, and that's true, but relationships without rituals can be shallow. Regardless of your ecclesial tradition, this book will help you draw closer to Jesus Christ, by helping you recover the timeless liturgies of the Christian faith, helping shape your faith and community in a time of spiritual angst. Damiani points us toward a more beautiful orthodoxy.

Read this book and watch God work in your own heart and in the heart of your local body of believers.

DANIEL DARLING, Director of the Land Center for Cultural Engagement and bestselling author of several books, including *The Characters of Christmas, The Characters of Easter, The Dignity Revolution*, and *A Way with Words*

This book has a permanent place on my bookshelf. As a tenured pastor, I'm worried how disposable our Christian practices are—short-lived songs, stream-of-consciousness prayers, forgettable sermons. I'm weary of fads. In our worship, both personal and at church, we need a sense of majesty, a connection with godly tradition, and enduring patterns to guide us from the secular to the spiritual. I'm not from a "high church" tradition, but how I need sacred elements to stabilize my scattered heart! Aaron Damiani's words have lifted me up. They'll do the same for you.

ROBERT J. MORGAN, author of *The Red Sea Rules* and *Then Sings My Soul*

If you feel hurt by the church or long to see, taste, and pray your way into real communion with Jesus, then read *Earth Filled with Heaven*. Father Aaron Damiani nourishes your soul with the simplicity and beauty of the sacred Scriptures, creeds, church calendar, and vintage prayers. In these pages, the shared sacramental life with Jesus Christ overflows like a thousand geysers into our world today.

BILL GAULTIERE & KRISTI GAULTIERE, founders of Soul Shepherding and authors of *Journey of the Soul*

The greatest promise of the Christian faith is not that we shall go to heaven, but that heaven is present here. In the raw, lovely stuff of which our world is made—water and oil, bread and wine, word and voice—God works and delights. No matter your tradition, your theology, or your tough questions, you'll find rich and honest hope in the promise of this book. Return here to our faith's deepest and most timely heritage—and rejoice.

PAUL J. PASTOR, poet and author of *The Face of the Deep, The Listening Day*, and *Bower Lodge*

For every Christian worshiper who is weary of simply going through the motions, Aaron Damiani has a bold suggestion: retrieve a sacramental vision of the life of the church. Pointing us at every turn toward Jesus as God's sacrament par excellence, Damiani helps us rediscover the beauty of ancient Christian worship in its life-giving rhythms and cadences: Eucharist, baptism, time, Scripture, prayer, mission. A grace-filled and engaging book for pastors, worship leaders, and lay Christians alike. Highly recommended!

TODD WILSON, President of the Center for Pastor-Theologians; author of *Mere Sexuality: Recovering the Christian Vision of Sexuality*

An increasingly frenetic and fragile world has many modern Christians desiring the old paths, the good way of our forebears in the faith, where the ancient practices of the church give rest to our souls as we journey to a kingdom that cannot be shaken. If that is your desire, then *Earth Filled with Heaven* is a book for you. Aaron Damiani writes with the gentleness of a pastor, the maturity of a seasoned sojourner, and the winsome warmth that comes from life-transforming intimacy with Jesus Christ along the way—from truly tasting and seeing that the Lord is good. If you are new to the old paths, Damiani will ensure that your first steps are steady and straight. And if you are further down the road, you will find him a most welcome and valued companion.

JOHN C. CLARK, Professor of Theology, Moody Bible Institute; author (with Marcus P. Johnson) of *The Incarnation of God* and *A Call to Christian Formation*

Liturgy, sacraments, the Christian year, creeds—for too long evangelicals have dismissed these as the stuff of dead religion. But this lovely book shows that, when founded upon a Christ-centered faith, they can become powerful channels of God's beauty, grace, and love, and antidotes to the bleakness of our modern life.

JOEL SCANDRETT, Trinity School for Ministry

EARTH

FILLED WITH

HEAVEN

FINDING LIFE IN LITURGY, SACRAMENTS, AND OTHER ANCIENT PRACTICES OF THE CHURCH

Aaron Damiani

Moody Publishers

CHICAGO

Edited by Annette LaPlaca
Interior design: Kaylee Dunn
Cover design: Erik M. Peterson
Cover illustration of icons copyright © 2022 by Bernardo Ramonfaur / Shutterstock (786091162). All rights reserved.
Author photo: Peter Thompson

All websites and phone numbers listed herein are accurate at the time of publication but may change in the future or cease to exist. The listing of website references and resources does not imply publisher endorsement of the site's entire contents. Groups and organizations are listed for informational purposes, and listing does not imply publisher endorsement of their activities.

Library of Congress Cataloging-in-Publication Data

Names: Damiani, Aaron, author.
Title: Earth filled with heaven : finding life in liturgy, sacraments, and
    other ancient practices of the church / Aaron Damiani.
Description: Chicago : Moody Publishers, 2022. | Includes bibliographical
    references. | Summary: "Earth Filled with Heaven is an evangelical
    introduction to the theological framework and habits of the sacramental
    life. Author and Anglican priest Aaron Damiani orients readers around a
    weekly celebration of the Lord's supper, water baptism, liturgical
    prayer, the church calendar, the daily office-rhythms that quietly
    nourish us with the life of Jesus"-- Provided by publisher.
Identifiers: LCCN 2022010122 (print) | LCCN 2022010123 (ebook) | ISBN
    9780802425362 (paperback) | ISBN 9780802476487 (ebook)
Subjects: LCSH: Christian life. | Spiritual life--Christianity. |
    Sacraments. | Liturgics. | Public worship. | BISAC: RELIGION / Christian
    Living / Spiritual Growth | RELIGION / Spirituality
Classification: LCC BV4501.3 .D3588 2022 (print) | LCC BV4501.3 (ebook) |
    DDC 248.4--dc23/eng/20220317
LC record available at https://lccn.loc.gov/2022010122
LC ebook record available at https://lccn.loc.gov/2022010123

Originally delivered by fleets of horse-drawn wagons, the affordable paperbacks from D. L. Moody's publishing house resourced the church and served everyday people. Now, after more than 125 years of publishing and ministry, Moody Publishers' mission remains the same— even if our delivery systems have changed a bit. For more information on other books (and resources) created from a biblical perspective, go to www.moodypublishers.com or write to:

Moody Publishers
820 N. LaSalle Boulevard
Chicago, IL 60610

1 3 5 7 9 10 8 6 4 2

Printed in the United States of America

To my parents,
Lou and Patti Damiani,
who taught me to love the Church.

CONTENTS

INTRODUCTION

BEARING FRUIT IN
A TIME OF DROUGHT

*How the sacramental life nourishes Christians,
churches, and cultures in a secular age*

The idea that Christianity could be "sacramental" might sound strange to you—even scandalous. What are your associations with the word *sacramental*? Perhaps words like *idol worship, liturgy, smells and bells, works salvation, praying to the saints, superstition, guilt,* and *dead religion* come to mind. Yikes. That's a scary list.

Here's a bold proposition: the best association for the word *sacramental* is *Jesus*. Yes, Jesus—the wonderful grace of Jesus; the glory of Jesus, His face shining like the sun; the life of Jesus, overflowing like a thousand geysers into our world.

You see, the word *sacrament* means *sign*—a pointer to a reality we cannot see.

On a recent bike trip, I came across a sign with the words *Deer Crossing*. The sign indicated that oft-hidden deer could lurch out in front of cyclists at random times, so I paid attention. The sign helped me orient my speed and raise my awareness.

If we're ready to pay attention, we'll find that life is filled with signs alerting us to a good, true, and beautiful Savior who is behind and above all reality. Scripture is full of those signs, and so are the historic practices of the early church. Followers of Jesus can deepen their own spiritual roots by paying attention and participating in those signs.

> Life is filled with signs alerting us to a good, true, and beautiful Savior who is behind and above all reality.

You might be, like me, an evangelical Christian. We believe the Bible is God's inspired Word, that salvation is a gift we personally receive by faith, and that works cannot save us. We are not interested in dead religion or idol worship. We are interested in the person and mission of Jesus, and we're curious to know how the practices of His earliest followers can root us more deeply in His life.

The sacramental life is a three-dimensional expression of God's nourishing, cleansing grace for us in Christ. On our way to see Jesus face to face, the sacramental life helps us experience His presence in a tangible way.

Maybe you feel run down on your journey of seeking Jesus. I often hear the words, "I've been hurt by the church," and there are so many variations on the stories that follow. Some are just exhausted by the church; the earlier draw of hype and excitement is now just wearing them out. Many with leadership responsibilities feel some despair when, after years of ministry outpouring, we aren't ourselves being refreshed by the living waters of Christ.

Others may be discouraged that our ministry or church isn't having the impact for which we've prayed and labored. It seems like the credibility and witness of Jesus' family gets worse every year as yet another celebrity preacher falls and yet another scandal reveals rot in the system. Unfairly or not, this trickles down to our local communities. Many of the people to whom we've given our love and life—especially the next generation—are walking away from their Christian inheritance altogether.

Others grapple with a "post-traumatic faith." Some of us trusted church leaders and have been burned. Others inherited a faith that blessed and burdened us at the same time. We love Jesus, but His people can be downright mean, even when they're trying to help. It could just be that the suffering of life outpaced the strength of our faith and we've yet to reconcile our scar tissue with the Savior's. We need to heal, rest, and process our trauma without pressure, hype, or formulas.

Most of all, many want to be faithful to Jesus in our generation, even as we witness growing suspicion and hostility to Jesus, the gospel, and the local church. We don't want to be reactionary, yet we are aware that the cultural forces often pose a temptation and a threat that call for a faithful, Spirit-filled response.

"Come to me, all who labor and are heavy laden, and I will give you rest" (Matt. 11:28). That was Jesus' promise to His earliest followers, and He's still ready to make good on His offer.

What would it look like for us to deepen our roots and tap

into an underground, ancient spring of our life in Him?

What would it look like for our faith to flourish in the harsher conditions, offering shelter to spiritual pilgrims looking for shade?

What would it look like for the church to not escape the culture, but be fruitful within it?

What would it look like to not abandon the grace of God, but to drink more deeply from it?

I am reminded of a promise God gave to His people in exile:

> Blessed is the man who trusts in the LORD,
>   whose trust is the LORD.
> He is like a tree planted by water,
>   that sends out its roots by the stream,
> and does not fear when heat comes,
>   for its leaves remain green,
> and is not anxious in the year of drought,
>   for it does not cease to bear fruit. (Jer. 17:7–8)

Maybe when the people of God heard these verses, they remembered the date palm tree, clustered as it was around water sources in the desert. "Don't be afraid," the Lord said, "if you are rooted in My life, you can be fruitful and bear fruit in a time of drought." Though their world was being turned upside down and all sacred spaces were profaned, their roots would draw nourishment from the life of God.

The secular age has left us with growing chaos, loneliness, boredom, anonymity, hopelessness, and polarization. It has eroded core commitments, broken bonds of trust, and left us with too many options and too little meaning. As we practice the sacramental life in the spirit of Jesus, we find that chaos gives way to meaning, loneliness gives way to family, and polarization gives way to peace. When secular life has eroded our humanity, practicing the sacramental life helps us recover it.

When we see the world as created and redeemed by God, we see it sacramentally. Our world, fallen and broken though it may be, is crammed with the glory of God. Even in the darkest corners, a hidden lamp shines.

> When secular life has eroded our humanity, practicing the sacramental life helps us recover it.

As we learn to rest under that deeply rooted tree, we pray for that day when the storm clouds of revival roll in, for the day when the desert becomes a garden once again, when the earth is covered with the glory of the Lord as the waters cover the sea.

At one of the darkest times in my life, it was the sacramental life that helped me see Jesus again.

1

MY STORY

THE WEARY AND THE HEAVY-LADEN

Strange as it sounds, it was Christianity that almost killed my Christian faith—not because it was so bad, but because it was so good. It excited me, taught me, challenged me, encouraged me, and put me to work for the gospel—until I collapsed.

I ran up all nineteen floors to reach my dorm room on my first day of Bible college.

As an eighteen-year-old freshman at Moody Bible Institute, I was thrilled to expand my horizons. For years I had been a frustrated extrovert in a small Ohio town, subsisting on a Bible church youth group and Christian radio. Now that I was in the big city, among peers who shared my faith and level of earnest desire to serve the Lord, I didn't mind the nineteen floors—not at first.

Whatever the evangelical college program was, I was there for it: the new friends, the daily chapel sessions featuring sermons from notable pastors, the Christian concerts, the Bible and theology classes, the Christian-themed improv group, the late-night conversations in the dorm lounge, the city evangelism and justice initiatives, the Cubs games and Chicago hot dogs, even the accountability partners.

For a while, everything worked. My professors deepened my appreciation for the Bible and awakened me intellectually. My devotional life only got better as a result. My peers provided the iron-sharpening-iron spiritual community. The worship and prayer nights stoked my passion for God. My head and my heart soaked all of it up like water and sunshine. I was growing. This was the Christian life, and I didn't want it to end.

For someone who came to faith in Christ at the age of five and grew up in a Christian home, this was perhaps the closest I came to a conversion experience. I give thanks to God for it. The joy and discovery of that season cut a deeper channel in my soul that remains to this day.

As the year drew to a close, my dorm leader took me under his wing and encouraged me to get involved in student leadership. There was a shortage of applicants for the leadership vacancies, he said, and I was mature enough to step in to fill the gap. I would learn later in life that there is usually a shortage of mature, capable leaders where they are most needed—and that need does not constitute a call. But at the time, I was deeply honored by the invitation. Who better to come to the rescue than me, the one who had the enthusiasm to run up all nineteen floors on my first day?

After being put into leadership, I poured everything I had into this opportunity. I prayed for God to give me vision. I made an elaborate, knock-'em-dead mural out of construction paper and colored tissue to communicate the vision. I spent time working the vision into a discipleship cohort of moldable freshman. I hoped to replicate in them the joyful experience I'd enjoyed the previous year.

And then it happened. I'll never forget the phone call from my close friend at the time: "Aaron, my dad took his own life." I didn't know what to say. I hadn't seen this coming at all. My friend's family had seemed so happy and healthy to me. They were committed Christians, involved in their own church. I had never heard much about Christians committing suicide. The reality of this death was like an intruder in my otherwise happy existence.

At the time, my friends and I had been attending a new, large, growing Bible church. The worship was upbeat, the architecture was innovative (church in a former warehouse? Cool at the time!), and our pastor had the "it" factor. He mesmerized us for nearly an hour each Sunday with his bold, in-your-face expository preaching. The services were like a roller coaster ride at an amusement park: they left us feeling thrilled, special, angry, tender, guilty, and loved—sometimes in the same service. We didn't always know what Sunday would hold, but it was bound to be interesting. Given how fast the church was growing, we carried this sense that our pastor would eventually get big and discovered, and then our church would get big and discovered, which would be even more exciting and special. We filled the huge parking lot with cars and the huge warehouse with people every Sunday, several times over.

Yet after the suicide, we didn't so much need space to park the car as much as we needed a space to grieve the loss. We needed a space to be still before God, free of unnecessary noise and provocative personalities. We needed space from the happy and produced experiences so that our messy and human experiences could run their course. We needed space not to have to feel anything at all—but simply to be welcomed into the presence of the Father, Son, and Holy Spirit.

Meanwhile, my coursework changed to a minor key. As I learned how the Bible was written, collected, and held together, I grew disenchanted with it. I began to stand over God's living Word, analyzing it from new angles, less and less interested in its power to refresh and convict. Even the tamest of exposures to postmodernism and critiques of the Christian faith—from believing, faithful professors—left me questioning all I had trusted. The more I learned, the less I believed. I felt like a bad Christian for entertaining these doubts and didn't share those concerns with many people.

And that's when the criticisms started from the ministry I was leading. I didn't have a healthy way to process the negative feedback. I could only feel the raw shame, fear, and hurt of getting dinged as a leader. "He's not investing in us enough . . . We don't like his vision . . . He's made some bad decisions." These words stung. *After all I've done to help and lead them!* I fumed to myself.

It seemed that the entire world I had flourished in was turning against me. Instead of changing course, I doubled down into more of the same: more quiet times, more worship music, more sermons, more ministry initiatives, more theology—more learning, feeling, and trying. My friend David, a former Christian college chaplain, calls this the learn-more-do-more treadmill. Struggling in your faith? Learn more. In a relational crisis? Do more. It's worked before; it should work again. It was like attempting those nineteen flights of steps, except this time I collapsed before I reached the top.

With my emotions fried, my thoughts confused, my energy for Christian service depleted, I was hitting a wall and experiencing a true crisis of faith. I couldn't feel my way to God anymore—not in my old way of doing that, at least. I couldn't think and learn my way to God through quiet times or theology books, and I couldn't serve and lead my way to God. Yet I longed for God.

> I couldn't feel my way to God. I couldn't think and learn my way to God. I couldn't serve and lead my way to God. Yet I longed for God.

Around that time my friend Phil invited me to a church called Covenant Presbyterian, a reformed congregation in Chicago's Bucktown neighborhood. Covenant met in a converted century-old Polish Catholic church building. It was austere—no statues of saints remained— with cracked walls and unreasonably stiff pew benches. Yet the architecture was beautiful and sturdy, and it lifted my gaze heavenward.

Within these old stone walls and old stained glass, I was given old prayers to pray. This is maybe the moment I learned that the church could be like a mother. Mothers tend to know what their kids need the moment they walk through the door: "Come on in. Here's a chair for your tired body. You must be famished; here's a plate of dinner. I've got your bed ready, but first, a hug. Bring it in."

I arrived at Covenant's front steps weary and heavy-laden. My mind, heart, and energies were all burned out. She welcomed me like a son to be loved, not a customer to be managed. "Here, try these prayers. You don't have to come up with new ones. They are all just Scripture, stitched together with prepositions. You don't have to feel them or even believe them at first. Just take your seat and pray with the family." In my state of burnout, I could receive a set of prayers as beautiful and ancient as the architecture. As I prayed, the prayers lifted my soul heavenward, too.

It's funny, I had always heard that liturgy and formalities in church were works-based salvation: an empty set of rituals that alienated people from the grace of Jesus. Yet for me, it was the opposite. The historic forms and seasons of the church, including the church calendar and frequent Communion, put the grace of Jesus on full display. It gave me a way to participate in that grace with my kneeling knees, my gazing eyes, my chewing mouth, and my praying voice. It was like that "easy yoke" Jesus talked about with His disciples. It fit, light and easy-like; the longer I wore it, the more I learned of His gentle and lowly heart for me—not just in my head, but in my muscle memory. My soul started to rest, week by week.

It might sound as if I'm describing the perfect church, but it wasn't. More importantly, the church didn't need to be perfect; perfect was what had exhausted me in the first place. I had begun to sour on perfect, produced, and passionate worship experiences. I didn't need the church

My soul started to rest.

to deliver premium religious goods and services in exchange for my tithe dollars (which, let's be honest, weren't considerable to begin with). I needed Jesus, in all His simplicity and beauty. The liturgical, historic forms of worship gave me Jesus. The sermon did not have to be the main event that draws everyone back the next week. The preaching could simply be the gospel verbalized, and the sacraments (the Lord's Table and baptism) could be the gospel visualized, working in tandem. And the church could be that mother with crinkly eyes and open arms, standing on the porch like Lady Wisdom, crying out, "Come and see the gospel! Come and taste the gospel! Come and pray the gospel! Come buy wine and milk without money and without price!"

Looking back, I was still a hot mess with plenty of issues. Liturgy is not a panacea for the human condition. But it's a start. I was like a sapling, already bent over and misshapen, lashed next to a giant, healthy tree, all the while being husbanded by the Holy Spirit. The roots would deepen slowly; the fruit would eventually appear. And my head and my heart would eventually catch up with my body. But first, I needed to rest, receive, and slow down. Liturgy—a central part of the sacramental life—helped me do that.

As I've talked to other Christians, I've realized I'm not all that unique. Even the most zealous believers slam into challenges, or seasons of doubt and dryness, that leave them aching for more. They need to rest and heal, recover their head and their heart, and in the process receive a new vision of Christ and His church.

Where can weary and heavy-laden believers begin to look for this kind of recovery? The easy yoke of the ancient church can strengthen our faith after the world, the flesh, and the devil have done their best to strangle it altogether. The church's creeds and calendar, the passing of the peace and praying old prayers, and even a few strange customs work together to create a pattern of worship and prayer that sustains the church's mission and a life of courage. A strong place to start is with the basics—the sacraments themselves.

II

EUCHARIST

RECOVERING OUR VISION
OF CHRIST AND CREATION

Let's get right to the point. What's happening at Communion (or the Lord's Supper or the Eucharist, depending on your church tradition), and why does it matter?

One of my parishioners texted me recently: "Isn't Communion *just* a wafer and wine? I don't get the 'something more' idea." To paraphrase Shakespeare: "What's in a name? A wafer by any other name still tastes like cardboard." If it looks like bread and juice, and tastes like bread and juice, it's probably not exactly Jesus, right? I certainly don't feel more spiritual in drinking it. And if I did, might not that become idolatry, where we worshiped the Communion bread and wine instead of worshiping Christ Himself? These are legitimate questions.

During their last meal together, Jesus took the bread in front of Him and said something extraordinary about it to His disciples: "Take, eat; this is my body." He raised a glass of wine and declared: "This is my blood of the covenant, which is poured out for many" (Matt. 26:26–28). Within hours, Roman soldiers would brutalize His body and spill His blood. But given His words the night before, we know He was in fact giving His body and pouring His own blood, for us, in love. He was the perfect spotless Lamb of God, who took away the sins of the world. Since that fateful day, billions of people have been made right with God through His sacrifice. In response, they have commemorated His death and celebrated their forgiveness in a Communion meal. But what exactly is the relationship between His body and the bread, or His blood and the wine (or watered-down grape juice)?

Some say that Communion is simply a remembrance. Jesus isn't present in any special way when Christians take it. Others contend that Jesus is present in an unseen spiritual way to people taking the meal. Yet still others believe that in addition to His spiritual presence, Christ is present physically in the bread and the wine, which become His literal blood and body. But is the bread *really* Jesus? Much blood and ink has been spilled in debate of this issue.[1]

Whatever your perspective on the Lord's Supper, what it is or isn't, I wonder if you'd be willing to do a thought experiment with me. Let's say you worked hard to make something beautiful or delicious or useful and designed it to express your love to someone you cared about. You poured your heart and soul into making this a special gift. Now imagine presenting your carefully prepared meal, drawing, bookshelf, poem, or rosebush to a friend, family member, or significant other. "Here it is! Isn't it beautiful (or delicious, or useful)?"

What if, in response, they shrugged their shoulders and said, "Well, it's just hot food on a plate." Or "Thanks, but isn't this just a scramble of words on a page?" Or "What's the fuss? It's just some wood and paint."

How deflating would that be? Rather than seeing the love and meaning you invested in your gift, what if all they saw was the bare visible properties? It would seem they had missed you and your love for them entirely, and maybe the most painful word in their response is the word *just*.

Theologian Hans Boersma once observed that the word *just* refuses to acknowledge the true depth and meaning of our world.[2] When the word *just* escapes our mouth, it betrays our true view of reality: cut off from mystery, without love, meaning, or intention, available to be exploited or discarded.

What if we took the word *just* and applied it to everything the Lord Jesus has given us, not just His Communion meal?

The baby growing inside your womb? *Just* a clump of cells.

The nature preserve with trees and wetlands? *Just* dirt and water, ripe for a developer.

The employees who work for us? *Just* cogs in our machine.

The vows we made for better or worse? *Just* words. And we were *just* kids when we said them.

The sermon from God's Word? *Just* a talking head.

The attractive young man or woman walking by? *Just* a body. And I'm *just* enjoying the view.

If these things have no purpose, no Creator, and no loving intention, they are "just" raw material to use or discard. This view of reality is more pervasive than you might assume. I wonder if we have a deeper problem than minimizing the Lord's Supper.

Consider the fictional example of Daniel Plainview, the oil tycoon in the movie *There Will Be Blood*. Early on in his career, Daniel adopted a toddler who was abandoned in a basket in the desert. He did this to craft an image of himself as a family man, in order to garner sympathy from landowners. Once his son grew up to become a competitor in the oil business, Daniel discarded him just as quickly as he had adopted him.

Use and discard.

Consider the sinister Cathy Ames from John Steinbeck's classic novel *East of Eden*. Loveless and cold, Kate exploited people's moral failings for her own profit and entertainment. After gaining control of a local brothel, she gathered incriminating evidence against the upstanding men of society in order to destroy their reputations. Her estranged husband, Adam, who discovers what she's been up to, confronts the condition of her heart: "The men who come to you here with their ugliness, the men in the pictures—you don't believe those men could have goodness or beauty in them. You see only one side, and you think—more than that, you're sure — *that's all there is*."[3]

But among all fictional characters, it might be Saruman, the turncoat wizard from J. R. R. Tolkien's *Lord of the Rings,* that takes the cake. Instead of seeing Middle Earth as an enchanted world with purpose, he saw it as *just* raw material for the expansion of his powers. In Saruman's estimation, hobbits are *just* halflings, of no value besides access to the Ring of Power (and their Longbottom Leaf pipe-weed, let's not forget). The Fangorn Forest was *just* fuel for his ever-churning factory. And people were *just* pawns to be manipulated in his war. In the words of Treebeard, the wise tree-leader who was once his friend: "He [Saruman] has a mind of metal and wheels; and he does not care for growing things, except as far as they serve him for the moment."[4] The result was devastation and despair for anything Saruman touched.

Daniel Plainview, Cathy Ames, and Saruman all missed the point of creation. Through their actions they were essentially saying, "It's *just* stuff for me to use, wreck, and discard!" To be honest, I've said the same thing through my own choices. Maybe you have too. "This thing has no meaning, but that it gives me pleasure, profit, or power." After using the thing, we toss it on the ground, or burn it, or cancel it altogether. And the trash heap piles higher and higher.

One real-life fallout of this use-and-discard approach was Patrick, a teenager caught in the cycle of human trafficking. By his own account, Patrick was generally looked down on as a kid. He was from the sticks and was held back by both a learning disability and a speech impediment. To the horror of his parents, he was snatched out of the safety of his home by a gang of traffickers. Patrick disappeared entirely. His captors snuck him across state lines and forced him to endless days of manual labor for their own profit.

This is the point where most people would be tempted to perpetuate the pain they have endured. Reading Patrick's story, I half expected him to become another Daniel Plainview or Saruman, another wrecked man wrecking the world. Yet something surprising happened for Patrick. Instead of giving in to the hate and contempt, Patrick turned to the God he'd ignored all his life. He had been raised by Christian parents, but Patrick had rebuffed the gospel until he found himself destitute. As he turned to Christ, the Holy Spirit flooded his young heart with the love of God. He realized that even though he was not of noble birth by earthly standards, he was created by the Most High. Patrick sensed that Jesus identified with him so deeply that when he was mistreated, Jesus took it personally.

This revolutionized Patrick's vision of the world. His imagination was baptized. If he could see Jesus Christ in himself, he could see Jesus Christ in the face of his enemies. He could see Jesus Christ in his land of exile. Even though it was a strange land and filled with cruel-hearted people, he became convinced that it was created by, for, and with Jesus Christ. So he began to delight in it. He made his work his temple, and he let the creation around him become a window for prayer and fasting.

By a literal miracle of God, Patrick escaped his imprisonment. He slipped his captors, caught a ride back home, and greeted an astonished yet grateful set of parents. They begged him never to leave again. He was relieved to be home. Yet one night while he slept, Patrick had a supernatural vision that disrupted his life again. In the vision, Patrick saw a man coming to him—from the country he had just escaped! The man was carrying a sack bursting with letters from the people of that wretched land. They were begging him to return, to live among them, to walk with them, to love them as Christ had loved him while he was a prisoner.

Against all odds, Patrick, later known as "Saint" Patrick, returned to the country of Ireland. The honor of his life was to evangelize the Celtic pagans—many of whom had previously treated him like discardable scum. He baptized all who converted in the name of the Father, Son, and Holy Spirit. In the process, he taught them how to see the world as he had come to see it: created by Jesus Christ, the Son of God who took on a human body and lived among us.[5]

Patrick's influence on the Irish imagination is captured in "St. Patrick's Creed," which extols both the majesty of God and the goodness of God's creation:

> *Our God, God of all people,*
> *God of heaven and earth, sea and rivers,*
> *God of sun and moon, of all stars,*
> *God of highest mountain, of deepest valleys,*
> *God over heaven and in heaven and under heaven. . . .*
>
> *He inspires all,*
> *he gives life to all,*
> *he surpasses all,*
> *he upholds all.*
>
> *He ignites the light of the sun.*
> *He surrounds the stars and tells them to shine.*
> *He makes fountains in dry lands,*
> *and dry islands in the sea,*
> *and stars to serve the greater lights.*
>
> *He has a Son,*
> *coeternal with him. . . .*
>
> *And the Holy Spirit breathes in them.*[6]

Here's what Patrick knew and Ireland discovered: the beating heart of creation is Jesus Christ. If you want to know the true purpose of a bird, or a springtime bud, or a baby girl, or bread and wine for that matter, look at Jesus Christ. Everything on earth was created for Him, by Him, and through Him (Col. 1:15–17). In the words of theologian Michael Reeves, "Jesus Christ, God the Son, is the Logic, the blueprint for creation. He is the one eternally loved by the Father; creation is about the extension of that love outward so that it might be enjoyed by others."[7]

> The beating heart of creation is Jesus Christ.

Are you near a window? Look outside to catch a glimpse of the sky. When you do, remember this: *that sky was created for and by Jesus.* Is there a person anywhere nearby? Without being too weird, look at that person's face. Remember: *the Father loves the Son so much, He was delighted to include this individual in that love.* Pray for that person to be adopted as a brother or sister in Christ (Rom. 8:27).

Finally, take a deep, luxurious breath, nice and slow. As you do, remember this: *this breath is a gift from Jesus Christ, generously given to me out of love. Even as I breathe, I can participate in that love.*

Jesus Christ identifies so closely with our world that He became part of it, even after we bent it to our own liking. He identifies so closely with fallen people that He immersed Himself into our existence. This is perhaps one of the deepest, most profound mysteries in all of Christian teaching: *God became human.* The Eternal Son became the son of Mary and Joseph. He cried as a baby, perspired in the hot Middle Eastern sun, ate fish on the beach, worked long days, celebrated at weddings and mourned at funerals, took afternoon naps, hugged His friends, and sailed the Sea of Galilee. He lived, and died, and was raised to life in a male human body.

Along the way, He sank into the muddy waters of the Jordan River, identifying with every sinner, being baptized by John the Baptist. Jesus became friends with lowlifes and drunks. In the eyes of many, Jesus was *just* a Jewish day laborer, *just* a Nazarene, and *just* the son of Mary, rumored to be born out of wedlock.

Yet contained within this humble man from the sticks was the fullness of God (Col. 1:19). At key moments, God the Father confirmed this with His affirmation: "This is my beloved Son, with whom I am well pleased . . . listen to him" (Matt. 3:17; 17:5). He spoke the exact opposite message of Daniel Plainview: "Jesus, you have ALL of me in you! You're the Son in whom is all my delight." In His human body, Creator and creature were unified, heaven and earth were joined, for the life of the world.[8]

Jesus created matter; Jesus became matter; matter *matters* to Jesus Christ. He expects us to value matter as much as He did. I am sobered by Jesus' preview of the final judgment in Matthew 25:31–46. His criteria for determining genuine faith have to do with food for the hungry, clothes for the naked, drink for the thirsty, and human interaction with those in prison. Suffice it to say, faith in Jesus Christ does not take us out of the world of food, clothes, drink, and conversation. Rather, it *transforms* the world of food, clothes, drink, and conversation.

What's more, Jesus so closely identifies with the hungry,

thirsty, naked, and imprisoned people of human history that He says, "Truly, I say to you, as you did it to one of the least of these my brothers, *you did it to me*" (Matt. 25:40).

I shudder to imagine someone raising a hand to interrupt Jesus on that day. "Lord, You are speaking metaphorically, right? How could I be literally feeding that hungry person and feeding You at the same time? That does not make sense to me, sorry. Aren't You concerned about idolatry? Were You expecting us to worship prisoners? I mean, aren't You overdoing it here with Your identification with Your creation? Give me a break; they were *just* a bunch of poor people!"

Yet Jesus insists: you truly were (or weren't!) clothing Him, feeding Him, and visiting Him. His identification with creation is so deep, and our actions in creation so consequential, that it has a prominent feature on judgment day. He wanted us to see Him in the eyes of the prisoners and hear Him in the growling bellies of our neighbors.

Can we see that matter *matters?*

Most of the time, our spiritual sight would fall short. Jesus predicted this way in advance.

This is the fundamental issue around our view of the world: Can we see Jesus Christ in creation, around creation, and through creation? Have our imaginations been baptized like Patrick's or warped like Saruman's?

Can we see that matter *matters?*

Let's return to the Lord's Supper. What is it? If we took a microscope to the bread and the wine, the microscope would not reveal Jesus Christ. Microscopes don't reveal Jesus, per se, though they can reveal the brilliance of His creation. The Scriptures and the Holy Spirit, however, reveal Jesus Christ, especially when the body of Christ is gathered in His name.

The Scriptures and the Spirit direct us to draw near to Jesus Christ as we celebrate Communion. At the very least, we remember His death for us: "This is my body, which is for you.... This cup is the new covenant in my blood. Do this, as often as you drink it, in remembrance of me" (1 Cor. 11:24–25). So let us remember Him. Let us see Him. Let us taste Him. Rather than focusing on the physical elements of bread and wine, we can let the bread and the wine focus our attention on Jesus: His love, His words, and His promises. He's with us, upon us, in us, in ways we cannot fully comprehend.

For all those who have been broken by the world, Jesus Christ draws near, as He did for Patrick on those lonely Irish hills. He's even closer to us than the bread and wine in our mouth as we chew and swallow. As we receive the presence of Christ, we see that despite our flaws and insecurities, we too were made by the Most High.

For all those who have broken the world, Jesus Christ's body was broken. His blood was spilled for everyone who has drawn the blood of their neighbor. By grace, the Holy Spirit is drawing the real-life Cathy Ameses, Daniel Plainviews, and Sarumans to a judgment-day-in-advance, where the Lord's mercy covers our sin, breaks our hearts, and gives us a new story to live together.

For all those who have lost sight of the true depth of creation, the Communion bread and the wine can become corrective lenses. As we ask the Lord to set them apart for His purposes, and show simple reverence in relationship to them, we let them train us for how to treat the rest of creation. The Lord's Supper can give us the Lord's sight: creation is bursting with the glory of God.

Peter Leithart connects the dots for us:

> Because we find joy in Eucharistic bread and wine, we also find joy in the plate that holds the bread and the chalice that contains the wine. We rejoice in the table and the pulpit and the windows and the paintings or banners. Dismissed from the liturgy, we go out in joy—to find joy in pots and pans, trees and flowers, mountains and sunsets, sleek cars and powerful smart phones, joy in a husband or a wife, children or siblings, friends and neighbors. We find joy in all God's gifts.[9]

"I am Saruman, one might also say, Saruman as he should have been," said the wizard Gandalf after his resurrection in *The Two Towers*.[10] Gandalf shows us what Saruman might have become were he to see Middle Earth as it really was. Gandalf knew the material of Middle Earth had a harmonious, musical logic to it. He treated the most mundane creatures, whether hobbits or trees, with great respect. Gandalf knew they contained a goodness, hidden at first, that transcended their usefulness to him personally. The result of Gandalf's reverence was the healing of Middle Earth: the creatures under his care blossomed and fulfilled their purpose in the story.

In a sense, all of us come to the Lord's Table as Sarumans and leave as Gandalfs. We are pardoned for the destruction in our wake. We are commissioned with new sight, a deeper reverence for the world we inhabit. We are filled with the Holy Spirit, who raised Jesus from the dead and will renew the face of the Earth. Thus, we are Saruman as he should have been—regarding even the lowliest of creatures with reverence, whether pre-born babies or immigrants. We bring to life what others have trashed, whether run-down apartment buildings or overused farming land. Because it's not just stuff, and we're not just pawns. The story of Jesus Christ is the logic of our lives. And the Eucharist, rightly celebrated, helps us see this rightly.

III

BAPTISM

A WATERLOGGED COMMUNITY
FOR LONELY HEARTS

Loneliness is like water. It shapeshifts to fit any life situation, filtering down into the vacant spaces of our soul where friendship and communion should be. Loneliness leaves us with waterlogged hearts that drip heavy with sadness. The irony is that the presence of other people can intensify our isolation rather than relieve it.

Luc Kordas noticed this firsthand when he moved to New York City from Poland to pursue his art career. He noted that

This feeling [of loneliness] is palpable everywhere in the city
... There are different shades of it: the loneliness of an Uber driver who fled Venezuela, leaving his family behind, who sighs with relief when I quickly switch to Spanish; the loneliness that emanates from the people I talk to on dating apps;

the loneliness of the middle-aged Ukrainian woman at my local supermarket, who tells me in Russian that I remind her of her son, who she left behind in a war-torn country and who she hasn't seen in two years.[1]

Kordas's essay struck a chord with me, in part because you could switch out *New York City* with *church* and it could still be true. Kordas writes,

> There are so many crowds in New York, and there are also so many lonely people. . . . So many people here are focused on money or their careers. It often feels like no one has any energy left for emotional conversation, for relationships. Although it isn't difficult to find company, many of the interactions we have with each other are empty and meaningless. It's easy to be lonely and anonymous in a city like this. It's easy to get lost.[2]

Have you ever felt anonymous at church? Sometimes people go to church to find community, but all they get in the process is a visitor's gift bag and a weak cup of coffee. You can stand inches away from a huddle of people in an animated conversation in the church lobby, and you may as well be a hundred miles away. It's one thing to get invited to the newcomer luncheon, and quite another to get invited into someone's dining room on a Thursday night, where the real community happens.

After a while, people stop trying, and who can blame them? Sociologist Philip Jenkins notes that in recent years there has been a spike in people who *believe* but do not *belong*. That is, they believe in the gospel of Jesus Christ in some measure yet have no church community to speak of.[3] How many women and men have trusted Christ to save them from sin and death yet cannot find a church to relieve even their isolation?

I remember feeling lonely in church. In contrast to the people already mentioned, my alienation was not due to any lack of warmth or welcome. I *belonged* but did not *believe*. My skepticism about the gospel kept me from full participation in the church I attended. My experiences and reading outside church left me skeptical about what we celebrated within its four walls. If you had asked me why, I would have responded with something like this: "I want to believe that Jesus rose from the dead and that Christianity is real, but I know too much and I've seen too much. I can see that others believe, but I cannot enter into the joy with them." It was a lonely place to be—surrounded by the faithful yet feeling faithless.

> I remember feeling lonely in church— surrounded by the faithful yet feeling faithless.

Sometimes the church holds us at a distance, and sometimes we hold the church at a distance. Either way, the distance remains, and we are not made for distance but for depth. We were made to enter fully into fellowship, the kind pictured by the disciple John, who rested his head on the chest of Jesus at dinner (John 13:23), or like Jesus, who rested His head on the bosom of His Father (John 1:18). Yet that level of intimacy seems so elusive. Why can't we exchange our mediated, sequestered lives for one of loving participation in community?

One reason might be our level of sophistication. Consider the case of Nicodemus. He was a man of high pedigree, not simply a Pharisee but also an influential man in his community (John 3:1). Jesus even referred to him as "the teacher in Israel," suggesting he had acquired a headliner status as a respected Torah preacher (John 3:10). What's more, Nicodemus knew people. His keen instincts for spotting anointed teachers lead him to say this to Jesus: "We know that you are a teacher come from God, for no one can do these signs that you do unless God is with him" (John 3:2).

If someone said that to me, I would be tempted to respond, "Why, thank you for noticing! That sure means a lot, coming from *you,* Nicodemus. I've always admired *your* preaching. You're the anointed one, make no mistake! But I suppose you're right." Yet this is the exact reason why people stay lonely: our conversations stay at the level of mutual flattery and small talk and never plunge the depths of the human heart and ultimate meaning. Jesus wants to move beyond sophisticated niceties to Nicodemus's heart and soul. He answers, "Truly, truly, I say to you, unless one is born again he cannot see the kingdom of God" (John 3:3).

Some time ago I heard my daughter singing a catchy song that she made up. It goes like this: "When you're born, you're a baby!" I know I'm biased, but I like this song because it's a plain statement of fact: when you're born into the world, you're a baby in that world. You don't come out of the womb as a high-functioning adult but as a crying, vulnerable infant. The same is true when you enter God's kingdom: all the layers of sophistication have to go. Only then can you start participating in the family.

Babies do not have a hard time belonging. Consider how much close community awaits a newborn infant, assuming they are born into a loving family. As soon as they pass through the birth canal, they are cleaned, fed, held, kissed, cooed over, and included in the family life. If they feel neglected, they can (and will!) cry out for affection, provision, and blessing. If you belong in a family, you're never alone.

But I wonder if we like our sophistication better. For all the belonging available to babies, there are more privileges available to us as free-agent adults. We can go where we please and meet our own needs and wants without being tied down to a family. By staying half-committed, we can be sought after and marketed to, and we can select friends, products, and commitments that suit our preferences—no strings attached—on our own terms and in our own time.

Sometimes we are lonely because we want to be *wanted*, but *we don't want to want*. We want dynamic and glamorous people to fall over themselves to include us. We want to be sophisticated adults who stay on the receiving end of invitations from people in the church without any vulnerability required on our part. It's much harder to be the one who *wants*: the one who owns their craving for friendship, their need for community, their heart-cry for a blessing from Christ and His church. Practically, this looks like breaking into the huddle of friends in the church lobby and introducing yourself, maybe even inviting yourself over for lunch. This would require becoming like a child, an infant.

But for some, the pain of loneliness teaches us to distrust our own sophistication. After a while we would rather be loved than flattered. Maybe this is what motivated Nicodemus to press further: "How *can* a man be born when he is old?" (John 3:4). Maybe, just maybe, Nicodemus is tired of being on the outside looking in. Maybe he is ready to go through that spiritual birth and enter the family.

So Jesus explains the spiritual birds and bees to Nicodemus: "Truly, truly I say to you, unless one is born of water and the Spirit, he cannot enter the kingdom of God" (v. 5). How is a baby made in God's family? According to Jesus, "water and the Spirit." Two elemental forces must be brought together—one earthly (water) and one heavenly (Spirit)—to make new life. The veil between the seen and unseen worlds must become thin enough for us to enter God's kingdom.

As the early church understood it, Jesus was referring to water baptism here. They saw baptism through the lens of Genesis 1, which describes how the Spirit brought forth God's creation from physical water. They also understood baptism through the story of the exodus, when the Spirit brought forth God's children using the Red Sea.[4] The Holy Spirit is like an artist that uses physical water as His medium. He loves using water to heal and re-create human beings, from the Red Sea in Egypt to the rivers that flow from the throne of God in Revelation 22.

Consider for just a moment how beautiful this image is: the Holy Spirit sets apart physical water to be a sort of womb for people who want to be born into God's family. Since we need water to thrive anyway, this is a gracious choice that God would encounter us through such humble, earthy means. Inside this womb, God the Spirit imparts new life and a new heart and gives us the identity of a true child of God. God brings holy and life-giving power to the waters; we bring childlike faith that He will meet us.

But in order for that water to become a womb, it must also become a tomb. By going down into it, we must renounce all sin and shed the layers of pride. The Spirit sets those waters apart to destroy and take our heart of stone, our old identity—all the calluses and layers and buffers that kept us from the love of our Father in the first place.

> The Holy Spirit sets apart physical water to be a sort of womb for people who want to be born into God's family.

We see this process of death and rebirth in the story of Eustace, a character in C. S. Lewis's Chronicles of Narnia series. When we first meet him in *The Voyage of the Dawn Treader*, Eustace is an entitled, sniveling brat. He finds himself sailing with Narnian companions on the Dawn Treader on an adventure he'd rather not be on.

On one particular island, Eustace wanders from the group and discovers hidden treasure. In the process of hoarding it for himself, he falls asleep and wakes up transformed into a dragon. His greedy and dragon-like inner character finally has disfigured his outer nature. As a result, Eustace the Dragon is cut off from the Dawn Treader community and in danger of permanent exile on the island. His loneliness, which becomes unbearable, finally breaks his heart. He sheds big, boiling dragon tears of grief and loneliness.

Aslan, the Great Lion from over the sea, finds Eustace and leads him to the top of the mountain where there was a pool to bathe in. As a dragon, Eustace can't fit in the pool, so Aslan tells him to undress. He sheds his skin, trying to shed layer after layer of dragon covering to no avail.

Later, Eustace tells the story this way:

> Then the lion said—"You will have to let me undress you." I was afraid of his claws, I can tell you, but I was pretty nearly desperate now. So I just lay flat down on my back to let him do it. The very first tear he made was so deep that I thought it had gone right into my heart. And when he began pulling the skin off, it hurt worse than anything I've ever felt. . . . It hurts like billy-oh but it is such fun to see it coming away. . . . He peeled the beastly stuff right off—and there it was lying on the grass: only ever so much thicker, and darker, and more knobbly-looking than the others had been. And there I was as smooth and soft as a peeled switch and smaller than I had been.[5]

Aslan then throws Eustace in the baptismal font, which stings and purifies him, before dressing Eustace in new clothes he will wear for the rest of the voyage.

Aslan's baptismal font was for Eustace both a tomb and a womb. Eustace flew up the mountain as a dragon and walked down as a son and prince in Aslan's kingdom. This humbling death and rebirth reflects the real-life process in the early church. After a three-year discipleship process, baptismal candidates came forward confessing Christ as Lord, and they went into the water tomb to be born anew. In the words of one theologian,

> During the early years of the church, people were baptized in tubs containing extremely cold water, so they would experience a physical shock to mark the spiritual transition. Taken

naked from the water, they were anointed with oil, wrapped in a white cloth, given a candle, and presented to the congregation as new human beings. They were like babes coming out of the amniotic fluid of Mother Church.[6]

Now you might be wondering, "That sounds gross and messy. Aren't salvation and sanctification a clean spiritual process? Why would the Holy Spirit use physical water like that?"

To quote C. S. Lewis again: "There is no good trying to be more spiritual than God."[7] In other words, if God created us to be both spiritual *and* physical beings, why would we separate the two? If He Himself took on flesh and blood to bring us salvation, why can't He also use water, bread, and wine in the process? Lewis again: "We may think this rather crude and unspiritual. God does not: He invented eating. He likes matter. He invented it."[8]

Think again about the kind of family life that heals our loneliness. It's likely to be physical and messy: crying tears, cooking food, scrubbing pots, changing diapers, visiting hospital rooms, confessing sins, exchanging gifts and hugs and apologies. "Messy" baptisms usher us into the "messy" body of Christ where our salvation is worked out in community. The body of Christ sweats, cries, bleeds, and sings because she is made up of flesh-and-blood women and men and children. And God said it was very good.

Lewis is right: God loves matter. And Jesus Christ loves the church, no doubt about that. But what about us? If the only lasting cure for loneliness was the messy, baptized family of God, would we take that option?

As painful as it is to be lonely, there is a pleasure in it. We can idealize relationships from afar. We can get caught up fantasizing about the kind of church or spouse or kids or friends who would complete us. We can stand above real churches, families, and small groups with our critiques. As painful as it is to be isolated, it comes with a nice perk: we don't have to do the hard work of grieving our ideals and expectations.

Anne of Green Gables is a story that begins with Matthew and Marilla Cuthbert, a brother and sister, trying to adopt an orphan boy who will help them around the farm. Matthew sets out to pick up the boy at the train station and realizes the orphanage has sent a girl instead.

Matthew and Marilla have to struggle with the question: Will we hang on to our expectations of adopting a boy, or will we accept the reality that we have an orphan girl?

Everyone who walks into a church with high hopes for a clean-yet-close-community will wrestle with a similar question. Will we hang on to our expectations for belonging, communion, and connection, or will we accept the humble reality available to us? Will we receive with open arms the "orphan girl" of the local church? For all her flaws and quirks, she is a gift from Jesus Christ.

In the story, Marilla eventually lets go of her expectations for an orphan boy. After she lets Anne stay, something slowly shifts. Marilla and Anne begin serving one another around the house and around the farm. On occasion their personalities clash, and they trigger each other. Sometimes they have to exchange apologies and make amends. They share meals around the table, day in, day out. Their relationship bounces around: warm, stormy, boring, laborious.

One day Anne falls off the roof of a neighbor's house. As the neighbor carries Anne's limp body in his arms toward Marilla, Marilla has a revelation: "In the sudden stab of fear that pierced to her very heart she realized what Anne had come to mean to her. She would have admitted that she liked Anne—nay, that she was very fond of Anne. But now she knew as she hurried wildly down the slope that Anne was dearer to her than anything else on earth."[9]

For all her flaws, the bride of Christ is so very dear. We don't always see it until it's too late—if ever. Like Jesus said, unless we become like newborn babies, we can't truly see God's kingdom aright. A sophisticated adult can easily detect that the bride of Christ is ornery and ordinary, but it takes the eyes of a child to see that she is also a beautiful and sacred mystery.

> For all her flaws, the bride of Christ is so very dear.

I wonder what was circulating through Nicodemus's mind when he brought seventy-five pounds of myrrh and aloes to bury the dead body of Jesus (John 19:39). Maybe, like Marilla, he had a sudden stab of fear that pierced him to his heart, that Jesus and His messy kingdom would have been worth a new birth of his own. I suspect, though I can't be sure, that he got a second chance after that first Easter Sunday.

As a pastor, time and again I have seen God use the local church to set the lonely in families (Ps. 68:6). The waters of baptism run thicker than blood, as some are fond of saying. What better arrangement than to have Christ as our older brother, God as our Father, the church as our mother, with siblings and godparents to share our table?[10] Yet you and I both know loneliness never quite goes away in this life, even for the baptized.

Before our loneliness is forever healed, we must pass through a second set of waters: the Jordan River, the biblical symbol for our earthly death and entrance into heavenly glory. On the other end of the Jordan are all the children of God, more dazzling than the most glamorous people we have ever rubbed shoulders with, and more loving than the most affectionate friends we've ever had in this life. God the Father is there, and Jesus our Brother is ready to meet us and welcome us at His table and dwelling (John 14:1–4). Dearly departed saints and glorious angels await our homecoming. In his lonely exile, John the Revelator could see them clearly (Rev. 7:9–17). With the eyes of faith, so can we.

No matter how lonely we are, these saints keep watch as our cloud of witnesses (Heb. 12:1). When we sing praises with lonely, longing hearts, the saints join our voices with theirs, along with the angels and archangels. Together with them, we worship the same Lord, we confess the same faith, we surround the same throne, and we stand in one baptism (Eph. 4:4–6).

I suppose there was never such a waterlogged community as the people of God. In such a humble, beloved company, we are never truly alone.

IV

TIME

FIXING OUR CLOCKS AND CALENDARS ON JESUS CHRIST

There's a strong connection between keeping time and keeping our sanity. Parents of a newborn often feel as if they are losing their grip on reality. They are caring for a precious human being who doesn't yet have any rhythms for life. Day is night. Night is day. "Lunch" happens at 3 a.m. To cope with it, a parent is supposed to "sleep when the baby sleeps." The things we do for love!

As the baby develops, the child will need to learn how to keep time. Not only will this bring relief to the parents, it will help the baby grow into a functioning adult. Ordering time helps all of us mature. While it begins with learning when to sleep and when to wake up, it also includes learning when to work and when to rest, when to speak and when to listen, and when to celebrate and when to mourn. Indeed, there is a "time for every matter under heaven" (Eccl. 3:1). The wisdom of Solomon, or lack thereof, often comes down to our timing. When we attend to it, time can be a wonderful teacher—even a parent—helping us grow up.

Our quest for control over time has complicated our relationship with it. We "race against time" to meet a deadline. We "kill time" when we feel bored. Instead of learning its secrets, we treat time as an enemy. We use technology, cosmetics, and relentless self-will as weapons of warfare.[1] Often we believe the only way to advance ourselves and feel in control in this world is to defeat time and to mask its effect on us. Yet to succeed in this gruesome task would be a tragedy.

The Lord intends to meet us in the limits and lessons of time. Whereas tyrants like Pharaoh formed slaves by blurring time's boundaries, God formed sons and daughters by setting apart the days, weeks, and seasons of the year for them. In fact, one of the gifts of the ancient church is a Scripture-based way to fix our clocks and calendars on Jesus Christ. When we recover that gift, we recover some sanity.

At least three spiritual formation questions relate to time, formed around our days, our weeks, and the seasons of our year. These questions get to the heart of our relationship with God and provide an opportunity to learn more about what we might call "liturgical time." These spiritual formation questions contrast sacred time (meaningful for eternity) with the secular age (which fails to give meaning to days, weeks, and seasons).

1. Do we approach *the day* as a race to win or a rhythm to learn?

2. Do we inhabit *our week* as if it were a prison or a cathedral?

3. Do we mark *the seasons* of the year as a consumer or a pilgrim?

The Day: A Race to Win or a Rhythm to Learn?

One of my favorite races to watch (not to run, mind you) is the Chicago Marathon. Tens of thousands of runners gather in Grant Park in the dawn of a crisp October morning, each wearing a bib with an identifying number in the front and a tracking chip in the back, so their performance can be tracked to the second. Before the race begins, the crowd of runners is abuzz with hope and anxiety, hoping to finish all 26.2 miles with a time they can be proud of. Spectators stand at the ready with cups of Gatorade and encouraging signs.

The race begins with the wail of an air horn. *Go!* Adrenaline and carbs launch the runners like rockets past the starting line and into the first mile of the race. At first they are bunched up, and no one can go as fast as they want. As the minutes pass, the runners spread out according to ability and training. The minutes turn into an hour, and then two hours, as racers pass through Chicago's iconic neighborhoods of Old Town, Lincoln Park, and Lakeview. By the time they get to the latter half in Little Italy, Bridgeview, and Bronzeville, the winners have shaken off the other runners. As they cross the tape back in Grant Park, some finish with pride and others with shame and disappointment. All collapse in exhaustion.

Does your day ever feel like a race to be won—or lost?

Your day begins with the wail of an alarm. Go!

You rise early with high hopes and a long to-do list. Maybe today you can finally make progress on an important project. Yet within minutes you already feel behind. There's a line for the bathroom, too little time for a decent breakfast, and the train is running off-schedule (or traffic is holding up your car commute). As your blood pressure rises, you instinctively reach for your phone to check your email. Big mistake. As soon as you open the floodgates, a deluge of requests comes through. One is an *urgent request*. As you consider how to respond, your phone dings with a text from a family member about Thanksgiving plans. Can you finally weigh in, please?

For the rest of the day, you put your shoulder to the wheel: meetings, projects, phone calls, shuttling yourself or your kids to practice, food prep, phone calls, chores, bedtime routines. All the while, you compete with the hourglass, racing against the falling grains of sand with your productivity. Sometime after dinner, the sun goes down and you collapse in exhaustion. The minutes and seconds continue to accumulate, but all you can do is veg out, zone out, peace out. Your to-do list is 36 percent done, 64 percent undone. Also, you forgot to spend any quiet time in prayer and Scripture. Don't you care about God?

I have had many days like this in my life, more than I can count. My self-justifying heart strives to feel secure by beating time with productive work. Yet this is no security at all. When we race against time, we eventually lose. The sand can always keep going, the seconds will always keep ticking—yet we were made to rest.

Have you ever learned a rhythm: clapping to a beat, dancing to a song, jumping rope? Rhythm contains a sense of joy and cooperation. Someone starts a rhythm and invites others to join in, not as competitors but as cocreators.

When we race against time, we eventually lose.

The first two chapters of Genesis describe the beginning of time more as a rhythm than a race: God creates, God observes His creation, God rests from His work. Evening flows into morning, like the slow inhale and exhale of a deep breath. "There was evening and there was morning, the first day" (Gen. 1:5). Then there's a second day, and a third, and on through the seventh, when God rests for an entire day.

Dorothy Bass captures the rhythm with her words: "On the beat, God creates; on the off-beat, God pauses to see that what has been created is good." She continues: "[When] our bodies move to [this] rhythm of work and rest" we are following "the rhythm originally strummed by God on the waters of creation."[2]

How can we learn that rhythm?

We *begin our days at night.* Instead of beginning the day with the alarm clock, we can begin our day at dusk with the setting of the sun. In keeping with the rhythm described in Genesis 1 ("There was evening and there was morning"), we begin our "day" with rest. The setting of the sun gently reminds us to put down our work. While this is not possible for some who work at night or who live in climates where the sun never sets (or sets way too early!), most of us can try some version of this.

Sometimes at our family dinner table, we light a candle to mark the beginning of the day. This simple prayer of light has roots in Jewish and early Christian practice containing psalms, prayers, the lighting of a candle, and an agape meal.[3] The Anglican evening prayer service contains a 1500-year-old hymn I love called "O Gladsome Light." It goes like this:

O gladsome light,
Pure brightness of the everliving Father in heaven,
O Jesus Christ, holy and blessed!
Now as we come to the setting of the sun,
And our eyes behold the vesper light,
We sing your praises, O God: Father, Son and Holy Spirit.
You are worthy at all times to be praised by happy voices,
O Son of God, O Giver of Life,
And to be glorified through all the worlds.[4]

Even as the sun goes down, we begin to celebrate that the light of Christ never goes out. Our work is ceasing, but God's work continues throughout the night: protecting, empowering, creating, and healing.

So we can begin each twenty-four-hour period with rest and ask God to keep working. In the words of the beloved nighttime prayer: "Keep watch, dear Lord, with those who work, or watch, or weep this night, and give your angels charge over those who sleep. Tend the sick, Lord Christ; give rest to the weary, bless the dying, soothe the suffering, pity the afflicted, shield the joyous; and all for your love's sake. Amen."[5]

As evening gives way to bedtime and we fall asleep, we put ourselves and our loved ones into the hands of God. Eugene Peterson captures how this works in the grooves of God's grace:

We go to sleep, and God begins his work ... We wake and are called to participate in God's creative action. We respond in faith, in work. But always grace is previous. Grace is primary. We wake into a world we didn't make, into a salvation we didn't earn. Evening: God begins, without our help, his creative day. Morning: God calls us to enjoy and share and develop the work he initiated.[6]

Have you ever woken to the smell of bacon frying and coffee brewing? Maybe some French toast or pancakes for good measure? I love this experience; it smells like grace to me. While I have been resting, someone else has been working on my behalf and welcomes me into the day with nourishment. This is a picture of how we can enter into morning prayer. Rather than starting from zero, we are responding to God's work throughout the night and throughout history to bless, preserve, save, and nourish us.

Morning prayer is a central part of the Daily Office, otherwise known as "fixed-hour prayer." This keeps the rhythm of resting and working going throughout the day, infusing our days with the grace of God. It offers boundaries of prayer in the morning (lauds) and the evening (vespers, the service of light mentioned above) with an option to pause at noonday and even a simple bedtime service called compline.

These times of prayer provide a space to stop your work, hear from God through Scripture, confess sins and receive forgiveness, and intercede for yourself and others using the Lord's Prayer and Psalms as a starting place. It can be as simple as praying a psalm. You can pray the Office alone, though it's even richer to experience it in community. The heart of the Daily Office is not legalism and rigidity, but an invitation for people from every walk of life to work and rest as God's creatures. It's the metronome that keeps us on beat with God's grace.

> These times of prayer provide an invitation to work and rest as God's creatures.

Imagine it: your alarm goes off, and you amble into the kitchen to prepare your coffee (or tea, or smoothie). With your drink in one hand and your prayer book and Bible in the other, you find a seat near the computer and log in to the morning prayer Zoom call with others from your church. You mumble a morning greeting with a smile and enjoy a few minutes of silence in God's presence together. The leader invites everyone to a liturgical confession of sin. The grace of God in Christ is declared; you're beginning your day with a taste of God's love for you. Together, you read Psalm 95: "Oh come, let us worship and bow down; let us kneel before the Lord, our Maker! For he is our God, and we are the people of his pasture, and the sheep of his hand." Yes, that's right. If you are in God's flock, you are in His care, no matter what stress or surprises find you today.

Volunteers read the Scriptures assigned for the day in the Daily Office Lectionary. Though your group is small, you are reading the same passages as Christians around the world on the same day. This leads into a unified confession of the Apostles' Creed, praying the Lord's Prayer, and open intercession for our life and world. You remember the needs of your family and community, like those fighting cancer or facing bankruptcy. Morning prayer draws to an end with the Prayer for General Thanksgiving, which captures our desire to bring glory to God the rest of our day—and days: "Almighty God . . . We bless you for our creation, preservation, and all the blessings of this life . . . Give us such an awareness of your mercies, that with truly thankful hearts we may show forth your praise, not only with our lips, but in our lives, by giving up our selves to your service, and walking before you in holiness and righteousness all our days."[7]

Imagine what your life might be like if God answered that prayer for you: aware of God's blessings, alert to opportunities He's sending your way, your whole being giving praise to God, whether through your work, rest, or worship. By learning the "unforced rhythms of grace" of fixed-hour prayer (Matt. 11:28–30 MSG), we can begin to discover that life for ourselves.

The Week: A Prison or a Cathedral?

In prison, life can be a drag, lacking joy and meaning and purpose. Prisoners understandably feel trapped and want to get out. While a prison break makes for a good story, usually their escape happens the legal way: earning parole through good behavior, serving out a sentence one day at a time, waiting patiently for freedom.

Sometimes we treat the week as a prison sentence: counting down the days until we are free. Once the weekend hits, TGIF! It's when life really starts: parties, leisure, sports, and fun. While some of us are tempted to race against time, others are tempted to kill time—perhaps because we do not like our jobs, our stage or station in life, or the strictures of school. Or we may actually be confined in some way—in prison or in a nursing home or long-term care facility. In any case, we want to escape so real life can begin.

I will never forget the last job I had before becoming a pastor; I was a receptionist. The hardest part of the job for me was the lack of freedom: I was to sit at my desk from 8 a.m. until 5 p.m. every day, Monday through Friday, with a break for lunch. If I wandered too far from the desk and missed a call, that would mean trouble. There were no windows, only a TV that played cable news for the entire day. My job was monotonous: fill the printers with paper, fill office supply orders, take messages, print out documents, and buzz in visitors. The Lord used this job to teach me humility and patience and confirm a long-resisted call to ministry. Suffice it to say that assignment *did* feel sometimes like a prison sentence and quitting after a year *definitely* felt like an escape.

Maybe time feels like a prison for you, whether you are bored and restless by your station in life or you're far away in a foreign land, on bedrest for medical reasons, or waiting out a mandatory stay-at-home order.

Writing for *Wired*, technology writer Adrielle Pardes captured the profound alienation from time during the COVID-19 quarantines:

> Our experience of time isn't just different because we are fearful or bored, cooped up or overworked. It has changed because we don't yet know what to measure it against. Coronatime has no scale. "Time" has become a stand-in for all that we cannot control. It is both the breakneck speed at which

things are changing, and the burden of how much is staying the same. *We are scared this might go on forever.*[8]

What if we inhabited our week like a cathedral instead of a prison?

Like prisons, cathedrals have walls and contain people. Yet unlike prisons, cathedrals are set apart to reflect God's majesty and provide a home for the soul. Prisons detain inmates against their will; cathedrals draw in worshipers of their own volition. In prison, time drags on forever. In a cathedral, time collapses: God's saving acts in the past, today, and the future present themselves to us all at once. The Spirit-filled Scriptures, sacraments, and stained glass make for one eternal moment in time.

The cathedral of time begins on the Sabbath, the Lord's Day. Jewish scholar Abraham Heschel calls the Sabbath God's "Architecture of Time" where worshipers "enter not simply a day, but an atmosphere . . . a foretaste of paradise." He noted that the first object to be called "holy" in Genesis was not a mountain or an altar, but the day of Sabbath: "It was on the seventh day that God gave the world a soul," and "[the world's] survival depends upon the holiness of the seventh day."[9]

Do you see the progression? God *made* the Sabbath holy (Gen. 2:1–3), and then He commanded us to *keep* the Sabbath holy (Ex. 20:8–11). It's our cathedral now, a gracious gift to steward, not for its own sake but for

> As we keep the Sabbath holy, God keeps us sane. We cease work, enter His presence, and recover our life.

our own survival. As we keep the Sabbath holy, God keeps us sane. We cease work, enter His presence, and recover our life.

Sabbath is a twenty-four-hour period to cease from our work—both paid and unpaid—so we can savor God's holy presence in our lives.[10] As we enter this cathedral of time, we exchange the to-do lists, emails, and laundry for resting, delighting, and contemplating the love of God. It's a day set apart that honors God and His creation. Sabbath is a day to worship God, enjoy soulful music, savor a delicious meal, talk with a close friend. At this stage of life, I like to celebrate the Sabbath with a nice long bike ride.

Dorothy Bass captures the relief of the Sabbath day: "All week long human beings wrestle with the created world, tilling and hammering and carrying and burning. [But on Sunday], let it be ... Celebrate it as it is and live in it ... [with] peace and gratitude ... It is right and good to remember that it is not [your effort] alone that grows grain, forges steel, feeds your family, fights injustice, teaches your students."[11]

Many of Jesus' early followers celebrated His death and resurrection on Sunday.[12] Early Christians understood Sunday as the "eighth day," the first day of the Lord's *new* creation.[13] On Sunday, Christ is revealed as the true Passover Lamb who was sacrificed for us, as well as the Bridegroom who has prepared a wedding feast for us in the future. He is the Lord of Eternity lifted up before our eyes; we are set apart as His new creation people.

How does this transform the rest of our workaday week? It revolutionizes our perspective. The image to keep in our imagination is a cathedral or beautiful church in the center of a village.

Even as we are sent from the cathedral of Sabbath, we keep it in view as we labor and love within the village for the next six days. The Sabbath serves for us a vision of what is true of our world and our work: holy unto the Lord. As Eugene Peterson reminds us: "Without Sabbath . . . the workplace is soon emptied of any sense of the presence of God and the work becomes an end in itself. If there is no Sabbath . . . God's work is either forgotten or marginalized."[14]

My lifeline during my year as a receptionist was the Sabbath. In the mornings, Laura and I would give each other a break from parenting and household responsibilities. I would use my time to take a walk, talk with a friend, or spend time reading and journaling over a cup of coffee. In the evenings we would worship at Church of the Resurrection in Capitol Hill, DC. I can still remember the vibrant community, the rich sermons, and the way the sacraments strengthened my faith for the rest of the week. God used the Sabbath to honor my life, dignifying my labor as a parent and as a receptionist. It was my north star, the steeple at the center of my week.

The truth is that the rest of the week I was not in a prison of time, despite my limits. I was in the cathedral of God's holy and loving presence. He was as present in my windowless, cable-news-playing work environment as He was in worship on Sunday. In that job I had an opportunity to love my neighbor, experience life in a post-Christian city, provide administrative support for policy research on cybersecurity and technology policy, and learn how to be a friend and pastor to people who did not trust the church. Even as the Lord gave me Sabbath rest, I could provide rest on a small scale for everyone who stopped at the desk with a problem, question, or desire to connect.

Please do not hear me laying more rules on you. That's the opposite of God's heart for the Sabbath! He has constructed a beautiful cathedral-in-time to take away your breath and your burdens. You can be free from the prison of meaningless monotony and ceaseless toil. By recovering the Sabbath, we can recover our sanity.

The Seasons of the Year: Marked as Consumers or Pilgrims?

Last Christmas, we were facing a global supply shortage. Even before Halloween, companies were alerting their customers to purchase their Christmas gifts immediately. Families sent around their wish lists early. Even holiday turkeys were selling out. In watercooler conversations throughout the week, I felt the collective anxiety ratcheting up: *Will Christmas be the same if we cannot buy all the holiday stuff we need?*

I love gift giving and feasting on Christmas as much as the next person, and I grow weary of tropes about Christmas being too consumer-driven. However, I can't help but notice that *celebrating a season* is marked by *consuming*: food, drink, gifts, clothes, decorations, and experiences. And it's not just on Christmas.

Think about the rest of the year. What seasons stick out to you, and how do you mark them? Here are a few common holiday pastimes from American culture:

- On New Year's Eve, people love to party. It's the last feast of eating and drinking, of apps and dips and kisses at midnight.

- On New Year's Day, hangovers give way to New Year's Resolutions. It's a fresh start, and people purchase gym memberships, home workout equipment, diet plans, self-help books, and a session with their life coach.

- On Valentine's Day, we rush to the florist for the roses and cards—or to the grocery store for comfort food to numb the loneliness.

- On spring break, we purchase an escape someplace more exciting—or wish we could.

- During the summer, we get out of Dodge and rent a cabin, a week at the beach, and some fireworks for good measure.

- Early fall is back-to-school shopping season! We celebrate this fresh start with clean notebooks, sharpened pencils, fresh outfits, new thermoses, and cool backpacks. If you love watching football, this might be a season for grilled meats, face paint, and scoring tickets and jerseys.

- In my subculture, late fall tastes like pumpkin: pumpkin bread, pumpkin creamer, pumpkin spice lattes, pumpkin candy, pumpkin pie, pumpkin costumes, pumpkin church, and pumpkin sparkling water. (The last two might be a stretch, but give it time.)

How do you mark your year? No matter what your list of yearly experiences and highlights are, pay attention to how much consumption helps you mark the seasons. We tend to place a high value on comfort, feeling happy and connected. Buying stuff gives us a sense of control over these experiences, and it helps us feel like we are participating in a larger story. But where is all that consumption heading, exactly? Are we journeying anywhere specific, or just enjoying life the best we can?

Many of these experiences are good. Yet I believe the human heart longs for something deeper than comfort and consumption. We would do well to mark the seasons of the year as pilgrims rather than consumers. *Pilgrims* might sound like the Mayflower to you, but those aren't the pilgrims I am referring to. Pilgrims are on a journey—a pilgrimage—out of the familiar into a place where they can encounter God.

> Pilgrims are on a journey—a pilgrimage—out of the familiar into a place where they can encounter God.

Usually there's danger and discomfort in the journey. But there's also wonder, and beauty, and an expansion of the soul.

A pilgrimage can be a literal trip you take, to the Holy Land where Jesus lived and died, or to hike the Camino Trail in Spain, or even the simple act of going to church to worship.

A pilgrimage can also be a metaphor for the Christian life. In the classic *The Pilgrim's Progress,* the main character, Christian, journeys from his home in the City of Destruction to the Celestial City on top of Mount Zion. In the allegory *Hinds' Feet on High Places,* a young, crippled girl named Much-Afraid is guided by her two companions, Sorrow and Suffering. They lead her out of her oppressive home in the valley up to the mountain heights of the Good Shepherd.

These stories help us see that the spiritual life is a journey from a narrow, unbelieving, constricted life to one of freedom and union with God. All Christians are on that journey, no matter what their tradition or culture. The Scriptures make it clear that we are not yet home, but we are heading there every day of our lives (Heb. 13:14).

One key way we can actively participate in the pilgrimage is by observing the church calendar, sometimes called the liturgical year. Like the Jewish people who made an annual pilgrimage to Jerusalem, each year we can journey into the story of Christ and His church, the mystery of the gospel, year after year. Each season brings us yet closer to the Holy City.[15] And pilgrimage transforms us in the process.

For instance, take the season of Advent, which marks the beginning of the Christian year. The liturgical color of purple, symbolizing royalty, serves as a visual cue for us to wait expectantly for King Jesus. Don't you long for justice, for the world to be made right? Deep down, many of us long for this more than cozy experiences or cool gifts. Advent teases this out by focusing on the second coming of Christ, the final judgment. One of my fellow pastors likes to say, "We're not pretending to wait for baby Jesus during Advent." Baby Jesus already came the first time in great humility. He has promised to return in great glory as a King and Judge.

Advent features the theological virtues of faith, joy, hope, and love. Prophets of judgment and hope like Isaiah, Elijah, and John the Baptist are prominent. They model for us how to wait for Christ's second coming in the same way they waited for His first coming. We channel our sadness and hope through hymns like "Come, Thou Long Expected Jesus" and "O Come, O Come, Emmanuel." Return, O Lord, and make the world right! You've done it the first time, and we pray and wait until You do it again.

After four weeks of anticipation, we arrive on December 25, Christmas Day. Historically, Christians have taken twelve days to celebrate. This gives us enough time to eat until we pop, shower gifts upon friends and family, and most of all celebrate that the light of Christ has pierced this dark world. The liturgical color of white (or gold) reminds us of the purity of the light of Christ. An old English prayer captures the spiritual intention of this season of joy: "Almighty God, you have poured upon us the new light of your incarnate Word: Grant that this light, kindled in our hearts, may shine forth in our lives; through Jesus Christ our Lord, who lives and reigns with you in the unity of the Holy Spirit, one God, now and forever."[16]

After a fortnight of Yuletide, we are ushered into the Epiphany feast and season. For at least one Sunday, the church features the liturgical colors of white and gold. Whereas Christmas celebrates the humble incarnation of Christ, Epiphany highlights the unveiling of the glory of Christ to the nations. Epiphany features outsider figures such as the Magi, who come from Gentile regions to pay homage to the Christ child. Many churches choose to highlight world missions during Epiphany. The people of God retell the stories of unveiled glory in Jesus' life and ministry: His baptism in the Jordan river, His first miracles of healing, and finally His transfiguration in the company of Moses, Elijah, and the three disciples. As we behold His glory, we find, like His disciples, that we are being transformed by His light.

You might remember that after Jesus' baptism and revelation as God's Son, He was ushered by the Holy Spirit into the wilderness for a time of spiritual formation, solitude, prayer, and spiritual warfare against the devil. This may be the most difficult and transformative part of the pilgrimage for us: the season of Lent. Here, we head into a forty-day wilderness retreat of sorts, when we prepare for Easter through an extended time of fasting, prayer, and generosity. The liturgical color of purple is back: this time it calls us toward penitence and sobriety. We want to be right with God, so we allow Him to purge us of idols, sin, and extra clutter of the soul that keeps us from the love of the Father.[17]

The final week of Lent is perhaps the most intense part of the pilgrimage, when we walk with Jesus through the final week of His life, known as Holy Week. Holy Week originated with Christian pilgrims who would make their way to Jerusalem in the first few centuries of the church.[18] Like these pilgrims, we engage in a three-dimensional way with the events of Christ's passion: a procession with palm branches on Palm Sunday to celebrate His humble, royal entrance into Jerusalem (featuring the color red, symbolizing Christ's passion), a foot-washing and Communion service on Maundy Thursday, and a time of repentance at the cross of Christ on Good Friday (back to purple). Many Christians choose to pray the Stations of the Cross during Holy Week, taking the opportunity to ponder and participate in the sufferings of Christ. Holy Week is a time to keep in step with Christ and His people. It's a prayerful, hope-filled, sober week. By following Him on the way to His cross, we learn to pick up our own and find that He makes it a way of life and peace for us.

After six weeks of fasting and repentance, we arrive on Easter Sunday, the high feast of the Christian year. White is back: Christ is risen! One of the oldest Christian services is the Easter Vigil, a midnight (or close to midnight) celebration of God's salvation purposes being fulfilled in the resurrection of Christ. During Easter we find ourselves on the Road to Emmaus. Eastertide is seven weeks of feasting, joy, generosity, and restored hope.

Eastertide gives way to three great feasts, all of them celebrating significant gospel realities: Ascension Sunday, Pentecost, and Trinity Sunday. My friend Scott Cunningham started a tradition a few years ago with his congregation (Christ Church Madison) that celebrates these feast days with creative outreach events. On Ascension Sunday, the Sunday of remembering Christ ascending to the Father's right hand, they host a churchwide kite flying day. On Pentecost Sunday, which marks the sending of the Holy Spirit, they have a huge community bonfire. On Trinity Sunday, which celebrates the beautiful mystery of the Father, Son, and Holy Spirit, they organize a square dance, complete with a caller.

The season following Pentecost is sometimes called "Ordinary Time," which stretches from late spring until the first Sunday of Advent, about five months. While the Feast of Pentecost features the color red (marking the sending of the Spirit and the birth of the church), Ordinary Time is marked by green, the color of growth and vitality. In this season, we walk a long obedience in the same direction, seeking to grow spiritually and serve our community for God's glory. Ordinary Time crescendos in late November on Christ the King Sunday, when we recognize that Jesus Christ is the rightful Lord over heaven and earth. What a proper way to end the pilgrimage!

The following illustration shows us the pattern of the Christian Year:

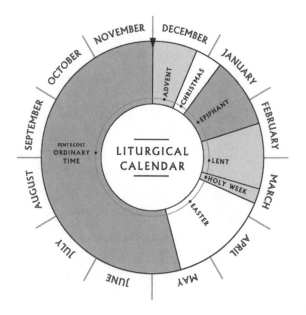

I have been taking a pilgrimage through the Christian year for about seventeen years now, yet I still find myself divided between my identity as a pilgrim and the control I feel as a consumer.

Have you ever traveled with someone who needed to control their traveling conditions? The temperature needs to be a certain level, the food needs to have a certain freshness, the seat needs to go back at a certain angle, the pillows can't be too lumpy, and the Wi-Fi needs to *stop cutting out!* Things need to be just so. I have been that person; maybe you have been too.

But if you insist on having control over all the conditions, you're not really on a pilgrimage anymore. This is part of why the liturgical year is so powerful: it yields control and calls us into deeper transformation. Every time we take the journey, it causes the shape of our life "to be curved into [a] script that proclaims [the] ... good news."[19]

Lauren Winner captures the longing that many Christians have when they begin to engage the liturgical year:

> One of my goals in life is to inhabit the Christian story so fully that Advent will be the instinctive beginning of my year. One of my goals is to inhabit church even more fully than I inhabit school, so that Advent hymns, rather than pencil tips, signal the beginning of the year. Why is this so important? ... First, I want the Christian story to shape everything I do, even how I reckon time. I want it to be truer and more essential to me than school's calendar, or Hallmark's calendar, or the calendar set by the IRS. I want the rhythms of Advent, Christmas, Epiphany, Lent, Easter, Pentecost to be more basic to my life than the days on which my quarterly estimated taxes are due. And ... most important: almost more than anything else I've done since becoming a Christian, trying to live inside church time has formed me ... in Jesus' story. Jesus drew my attention to himself, and the church calendar has kept it fixed there—on him. Church time has offered me the chance to reprise and reiterate Jesus' life every year.[20]

In the hands of God, time can again be our teacher. It's no good to fight it, kill it, race against it, or numb ourselves from its march. We may as well receive our days, weeks, and seasons as good gifts from the Father. We may as well let our "mother" church hold us while we kick and scream, while she patiently teaches us to keep time, and with it our sanity.

V

SCRIPTURE, CREEDS, AND OLD PRAYERS

STABILITY FOR UNCERTAIN TIMES

For all its conveniences and wonders, modern life can be deeply unstable. Technology has both accelerated and unsettled human civilization. Novel ideologies leave many questioning what it means to be a human being or an authentic follower of Jesus. Families are breaking up while tribes are forming. More than ever before we seem to have more stuff but less peace, more knowledge but less truth, and more connection but less unity.

On a personal level, change can disrupt our status quo without any warning. Imagine with me some typical examples of how this can unfold for followers of Jesus.

Earthquakes of Change

Mary has lived in a tight-knit neighborhood for most of her life, as did her parents and grandparents. Mary is a widow who lost her husband to heart disease and her best friend to cancer within the span of eight months. Yet she remains a faithful member of her church, a loyal citizen who gives back to the community, a mentor, a friend, and an example to many. All around her Mary notices signs of decline: the largest employer in the area relocated, as have most of the young people. Drug houses and decay have taken up residence where neighborhood children used to play. Mary grieves that so much she has invested in now has an uncertain future. Even while she sings "Great Is Thy Faithfulness" at church, Mary wonders why God doesn't preserve what is being wiped away in her life and in her town.

Jeremiah graduated from college three weeks ago and is ready to launch a career and a new stage of life. As he unpacks the last box in his apartment, his phone rings with his dad on the caller ID. "Jeremiah, your mother and I are getting a divorce. Please don't worry. We want this to be an amicable process, and we both love you. It's for the best." Jeremiah is crushed. He knew his parents had conflicts like every other couple, but they were seeing a Christian counselor. His soul feels torn. His mind spins with new and terrifying questions: Can he ever truly go home again? What will Christmas gatherings be like? Will his parents still support him financially? Jeremiah was ready for change and risk, but now he's looking for firm and solid ground to place his feet.

Corey and June are leaders in their local church. They started attending years ago as students at the nearby university. It was here they came to faith, got married, started their family, and put down roots. Now they help lead the thriving college ministry and host a small group of international students in their home. About a year ago, their pastor began to preach sermons that suggested a fundamental shift in his theology. The college students in the church appreciate the change with enthusiasm, but the elder board and other leaders have serious concerns. Without warning, the church they love is divided over theology, and Corey and June feel caught in the middle. On the one hand, they want to care for their students and support their pastor. On the other hand, they are concerned about sound theology and the long-term health of their beloved church.

I feel the instability in my own life. As a pastor in the city of Chicago, I am concerned about the loss of sacred spaces where Christians can worship on Sundays. Walking around Chicago in recent years, I have sometimes caught sight of a beautiful church. Often there will be a cornerstone with the year of consecration, like 1871 or 1922. But when I look toward the entrance, I see a row of apartment buzzers right where the church name should be. What used to be a living, breathing gospel community for the city I love is now gone. The building was sold for its parts to the highest bidder.

This impacts me practically. Our church needs a space to worship on Sundays. After the recent pandemic hit, we lost access to the school where we met. The Lord provided a new space, and the building we worship in is now under contract with a developer. I recently got troubling news that the sale may be completed within weeks or months, and we may need to find a new space. I can still remember feeling the anxiety in my body at the breakfast table:

Where will we meet? What will this instability do to our church that has already endured so much upheaval?

Praying Old Prayers

After breakfast, I did what I have learned to do on good days and bad: draw upon old prayers from the suffering saints of the past. I drove to the building where we currently worship, took out my Anglican *Book of Common Prayer*, and prayed the Morning Prayer liturgy as I walked around the church. Sure, I was praying that the doors of this building would remain open to us indefinitely. But the Scriptures assigned for morning prayer that day helped root me in something more solid: "O God, my heart is fixed, my heart is firmly fixed; I will sing and give praise with the best that I have."[1]

My emotions were not fixed—they were swirling with anxiety. My situation was not fixed—and it still isn't. But somehow by praying this old psalm, my heart began to fix itself on the solid ground of God's kingdom. It continues: "I will give thanks unto you, O Lord, among the peoples . . . for the greatness of your mercy reaches to the heavens, and your faithfulness to the clouds. Exalt yourself, O God, above the heavens; let your glory be over all the earth!"[2]

I remember praying those words while walking the concrete sidewalk toward Lake Michigan, looking up at the clouds, thinking: "Yes, Lord, more than a building for our church, I want Your name exalted in this city and Your Son enthroned in the hearts of the people who live here." I was reminded of the times God provided meeting space for our church in times past. Ever so slightly, I felt my anxiety go down and my hope go up.

There's just something about those old prayers, isn't there? The prayers with the longest shelf life seem to come from the saints who suffer the most. The texture of their faith is etched into their songs and laments, their supplications and poems. They stand like war monuments in a park, ignored when we are young and carefree, yet treasured once we have personally suffered loss.

Horatio Spafford was a successful attorney in Chicago with significant real estate investments in the city. He had so much going for him: a happy family, a thriving career, and a strong personal faith in Christ during the Chicago revivals led by D. L. Moody. But then the great Chicago fire of 1871 consumed most of his wealth, and soon after his four-year-old son died from scarlet fever.

Exhausted from grief and overworked, he took his wife and four daughters to Europe for rest and spiritual renewal. He sent them ahead on an advance ship while he attended to a final work obligation. To his horror, Horatio received news that their ship was sunk from a collision with an iron sailing vessel, and all four of his daughters perished in the Atlantic waters.

From the devastation of his losses came these words:

When peace like a river attendeth my way,
When sorrows like sea billows roll;
Whatever my lot, Thou hast taught me to say,
"It is well, it is well, with my soul."[3]

How many countless saints have sung the prayer of "It Is Well with My Soul" during their darkest and deepest trials and found their souls strengthened, consoled, and stabilized? Yet this hymn is just one of many old prayers available to us. What if, in a time of g.eat change and disruption, our prayer and worship life became more rooted, ancient, and filled with prayers from Scripture?

This is one reason why the ancient forms of prayer are a timely gift. Prayer books such as *The Valley of Vision*, *The Lutheran Book of Prayer*, and *A Prayer Book for Orthodox Christians* all take great pains to weave Scripture and sturdy-making supplications into everyday life. We Anglicans use the *Book of Common Prayer*, which contains prayers for morning, noonday, evening, and bedtime (compline). One of my favorite prayers from compline was discovered in a bundle of prayers from the early seventh century[4]: "Be present, O merciful God, and protect us through the hours of this night, so that we who are wearied by the changes and chances of this life may rest in your eternal changelessness; through Jesus Christ our Lord, Amen."[5]

> What if, in a time of great change and disruption, our prayer and worship life became more rooted, ancient, and filled with prayers from Scripture?

I don't know what challenges the author of that prayer faced in his or her life. But when I hear that prayer, I hear the heart-cry of someone who just needed to sleep in peace after a harrowing and anxious day. Like the person who wrote this prayer, most nights I find myself wearied by the changes and chances of this life, needing to rest in the eternal changelessness of Jesus, who is the same yesterday, today, and forever. Upheaval isn't going anywhere, and neither is Jesus.

Stabilizing the Tent

In the fall of 1911, my great-grandfather Benjamin Guthrie Fay attended a Billy Sunday tent revival meeting with a few of his friends. He was sixteen, the handsome son of a bank president and part of a clique of well-to-do young adults who had come to see the spectacle before it left town. Billy Sunday's revival meetings had a reputation for converting the down-and-out of society. Onlookers like my great-grandfather and his friends tended to sneer at the way the fiery, charismatic preacher would stage-act fights with the devil and preach at a high vocal register.

> I find myself needing to rest in the eternal changelessness of Jesus, who is the same yesterday, today, and forever.

Yet when it came time for the altar call, something unexpected happened. One of his female admirers teased my great-grandfather: "Are you going forward, Guthrie?" He responded, "I am a Christian." At that moment, the Holy Spirit devastated him with these words: "You are not a Christian; you are merely a churchgoer." So with that my great-grandfather walked the famous sawdust trail and surrendered his life to Jesus, lock, stock, and barrel. He would go on to study at Moody Bible Institute and spend forty-nine years as a missionary in South America.

Despite his flaws, I am grateful for Billy Sunday's revival ministry. God used him to make a positive impact on my family's spiritual history. The same could be said for other ministries built around the gifts of a talented preacher or Bible teacher, from the golden-mouthed John Chrysostom to Charles Spurgeon to the pastors harnessing technology for the gospel. Powerful preaching from the Scriptures can change many lives in dramatic ways. In fact, you can grow large churches around the preaching gifts of one person.

But talented preaching on its own cannot stabilize a church, any more than a canvas tent can provide long-term shelter and security for a crowd. That's far too much pressure on the Bible teacher. If they lack the hidden inner life of integrity necessary to sustain a public platform, great harm is almost inevitable. If their theological views begin to shift away from key doctrinal truths, they can take their followers down that same path. This is true not only for sermons, but also for books, podcasts, and videos—anywhere the Bible and theology is taught.

Good preachers are wonderful and necessary. They announce Christ's reign and apply His teachings to the challenges we face. My best labor goes toward preaching and raising up the next generation of preachers. Yet our faith in Christ cannot rest upon a favorite preacher. Neither can our churches. We need to recover the ancient, stabilizing pillars that have sustained Christians and

> We need to recover the ancient, stabilizing pillars that have sustained Christians and churches in Jesus Christ throughout history. We might call this "a solid architecture for a secure faith."

churches in Jesus Christ throughout history. We might call this "a solid architecture for a secure faith."

The Public Reading of Scripture

Until recently, Christians have always read, sung, and prayed Scripture publicly. This practice grew naturally out of the practices of the Jewish synagogue, where the Torah was read for the spiritual benefit of all worshipers. After Christ's ascension, His followers continued reading from the Law, Prophets, and Psalms, and added in readings from the Gospels and Epistles.

Where do we see this in Scripture and church history? For starters, the apostle Paul enjoined Timothy to "devote yourself to the public reading of Scripture" for the church in Ephesus (1 Tim. 4:13). As early as AD 150, Scripture reading was included in the order of service.[6] One church historian re-creates the moment for us:

> A reader takes up the Scripture, reading clearly, so that the people can hear, and efficiently, so as not to take too long. The people, many of whom are illiterate, probably listen closely and attempt to memorize passages of the Scriptures. The "president" of the community then gives a talk in which he applies the passages that have just been read to the lives of the believers.[7]

Imagine it—a mere one hundred years after the death and resurrection of Jesus, His people gathered every week to drink in the pure words of God together. Illiterate women and men yearned to hear the words they could not read themselves.

The Jerusalem Liturgy of AD 385 included a series of Scripture readings, the Gospels being the most prominent.[8] Each of the Reformers treasured this gift in their orders of service, from Calvin to Luther to Zwingli, from Hubmaier the Anabaptist to Cranmer the Anglican. It was such a basic Christian practice that no one left it out.

What's more, Scripture was woven into the songs, prayers, and liturgies. This makes sense, given that Scripture includes so many worthy songs and prayers! So no matter what temptations or sorrows people faced during the week, on Sundays (or whenever they gathered) they could expect to hear, pray, and even sing God's Word. These Scriptures would provide the ballast they needed to fulfill their calling. Singing leads to memorizing. Memorizing leads to more singing—as anyone who has had a song stuck in their head can testify. Wouldn't you like Scripture stuck in your head?

Notice that the public reading of Scripture is distinct from the sermon. I love sermons, both giving them and receiving them. Preaching is, rightly, a key feature of Christian worship. Yet in many evangelical churches, the sermon *about* the Scripture edges out the reading *of* Scripture itself. Maybe this is because we're not there to hear and recite the Bible, but we're there to hear the preacher. Sometimes we're drawn to a speaker's brilliant and surprising insights about the Bible that no one else has recognized before. Or maybe it's a preacher's powerful, sound, trustworthy exposition. Often we want the preacher to speak into our hurts, doubts, and hopes. In any case, reading Scripture takes time, and singing the Scriptures takes energy. So we scrap it to get to the "good stuff."

But quite frankly, Scripture *is* the good stuff. That is why sermons are devoted to explaining them and applying them. When we read Scripture publicly, we actually let God do the preaching.

> Scripture in the bones is like white cells in the bloodstream, providing health and strength from the inside out.

Faithful resilience means that God's Word shapes the rank and file; we all need to be reading it, hearing it, singing it, and praying it on a regular basis. Scripture in the bones is like white cells in the bloodstream, providing health and strength from the inside out.

The Lectionary

A lectionary provides readings from Old Testament, New Testament, Psalms, and Gospels for each Sunday throughout the year, as well as for special "holy days" such as Easter, Pentecost, and Christmas. The benefit of following a lectionary is that it ensures a steady diet of publicly read Scriptures, helps us track with the church calendar, and provides some cohesion with other churches who are reading the same Scriptures. At Immanuel Anglican we use the lectionary provided by the Anglican Church in North America.

The lectionary is not to be confused with the Daily Office, which provides Scripture readings for morning and evening prayer during the week.[9]

The Ancient Creeds

Nothing can destabilize us like disinformation. Have you ever experienced this? One news outlet or trusted voice makes an important claim. Yet that claim is disputed by experts, who offer new data. At that point, several people we trust on social media share a compelling essay that offers a third view, shining new light on the matter. People begin taking sides and getting into heated arguments. The aggressive tone makes it harder for us to calmly separate fact from fiction. Who is telling the truth, and who is manipulating us? Since no one can agree on a basic set of facts, we cannot take unified action. We are left with confusion in our hearts, division in our families, and chaos in our society at large.

If disinformation has rocked your world, take heart. The early church dealt with this in spades. What's more, God brought something beautiful out of the painful chaos of those early years. This gift is the ancient creeds—the Apostles' Creed, the Nicene Creed, and the Athanasian Creed. These statements of theological facts are true and beautiful, and they honor God's name. They kept the early Christians unified and on mission, and they can stabilize us today.

Soon after the birth of the church, people started spreading ugly rumors about God Himself. Some would-be leaders and teachers started whisper campaigns about the Father, Son, and Holy Spirit, as well as about the precious gospel of grace. It may surprise you to know that no one is more maligned and lied about than God Himself, and why not? The nature of God determines how we see the world, ourselves, and ultimate reality. If you can manipulate people's understanding of God, you can exercise power over other parts of their lives too.

Take God the Father, for starters. Unscrupulous people spread an ugly rumor that God the Father never intended to create physical matter. They suggested that this messy, bloody world was more or less an accident. God is not personally invested in physical matter, the logic went, so He delegated it to a rabble of other gods whose appetites and egos require our solicitous attention. God the Father *really* intends that we figure out a way on our own to ascend into a higher spiritual plane. In the meantime, we can do our best to avoid pain and seek pleasure.[10]

This lie appealed to the early church for at least three reasons. First, it gave them tacit permission to avoid persecution by participating in the local pagan ceremonies. If this world is run by other gods, it made sense to appease them and local rulers— God wouldn't care. Second, it meant they could ease up on other restrictions, like caring for the poor, loving their enemies, and observing sexual morality. Finally, it resolved a tension at the heart of the Christian faith: the reality of a sovereign God and the existence of evil and suffering. If God didn't create this world, there's no such tension.

That doesn't sound like much of a Father, does it? If God doesn't delight in the world, He surely doesn't delight in us, what with our gross, dying, accidental bodies. Plus, the God represented here had left us to fend for ourselves before the malignant gods and the chaos of the world. Unfortunately, this lie spread like gangrene and led to chaos and despair.

This is why the early pastors of the church required all baptismal candidates to answer this question directly before getting plunged into the icy waters: "Do you believe in God the Father

Almighty, Creator of Heaven and Earth?"[11] Notice how specific this question was: God is a Father, not a distant deadbeat. He's almighty, reigning over all spiritual powers without rival. God created both heaven and earth, so He is personally invested in our world and our lives. These truths about God the Father, so compact and clear, can revolutionize your life. Do you believe this?

"I believe!" This was the first part of the good confession, and down the baptismal candidates plunged into the icy waters.[12]

Another notable lie in the early church was that Jesus was not truly a man. Sure, they claimed, He was divine. But this nonsense about being enfleshed in actual skin and bones and blood was for the naïve simpletons. Some heretics even suggested that the apostles, who preached the incarnation publicly for the masses, passed on secret knowledge to the "spiritually elite" (you know, the people who could handle sensitive information): "Jesus did not actually suffer on the cross and die. That was someone else, you see, because why would the Lord subject Himself to that? And come to think of it, why should you? If Jesus didn't bear the cross and all that comes with it, you can avoid the nasty splinters of your own rugged cross. Join the secret inner ring of the spiritually elite, ditch your suffering neighbors, and worship a non-fleshy Christ."

Unfortunately, many early Christians fell for this seduction.

Yet Christ's incarnation—His taking on human flesh—was one of His greatest, most magnificent achievements. It is *good* news to our ears, not bad news. When Christ took on flesh, He reaffirmed God's personal investment in this world. As church father Gregory of Nazianzus reminded us, that has implications for every dimension of our otherwise broken, unstable lives: "For that which He [Jesus] has not assumed He has not healed; but that which is united to God is also being saved."[13] Without Jesus taking on our human life, He could not have healed it.

And where would we be without the cross of Christ? It stands at the center of the kingdom of God, making a way for us to be forgiven, redeemed, and made holy in God's sight. No suffering of ours in this life need threaten us anymore because the love of Christ has plumbed its depths, its heights. So as we bear our cross, He bears us. He has taken our greatest enemy—death—and made it the very gateway of life.

So the second question for baptismal candidates concerned the historic, enfleshed, suffering story of Jesus: "Do you believe in Christ Jesus, the Son of God, who was born of the Holy Spirit and Mary the virgin and was crucified under Pontius Pilate and was dead and buried and rose on the third day alive from the dead and ascended in the heavens and sits at the right hand of the Father and will come to judge the living and the dead?"[14]

"I believe!"

The final blasphemous lie concerns God the Holy Spirit. This lie may sound familiar to your ears because, well, it's a devastating power move: "I have the Holy Spirit, and you don't. He speaks through me, not the rest of you." This lie suggests that I am more anointed than the collective people of God, standing above other Christians. From my individual perch, I can look down on other people, make up my own rules, weaponize my feelings, elevate my experience of God as normative, and speak for God while ignoring Scripture. Rather than speaking through and supporting *the church*, the Holy Spirit's voice calls me away from her—so the deception goes. This particular deception created new divisions within the early church.[15]

Yet we know from Scripture that the Holy Spirit is sent from God to create His church (Acts 2:1–11) and unify her in truth: do everything you can "to maintain the unity of the Spirit in the bond of peace. There is one body and one Spirit—just as you were called to the one hope that belongs to your call" (Eph. 4:3–5). The Holy Spirit speaks through His people, and as He does He unifies those people in a way that is supernatural and a sign of the kingdom to come.

So the third question presented to all baptismal candidates concerned the Holy Spirit's vital connection to the church: "Do you believe in the Holy Spirit and the holy church and the resurrection of the flesh?"[16] Those who said, "I believe" were submerged for a third time, completing the rite. They confessed their belief in the Holy Spirit and the communion of the saints in the same breath.

These early baptismal confessions formed the basis for the Apostles' Creed, which in turn provided solid ground for the Nicene and Athanasian Creeds. What began as a simple Christ-centered confession in the first century that "Jesus is Lord" grew in the second century to a three-part baptismal formula we noted above, known as a "Rule of Faith."[17] With each challenge to God's nature, the creeds grew in length and specificity.[18]

One way to understand this process is how our body's immune system works: it grows stronger through challenge. When viruses invade the body and make it sick, the immune system dispatches the threat and organizes a resistance to it.

Heresy is like a virus to the church. When we lie about God, pain and destruction follow. This is what C. Fitzsimmons Allison called "the Cruelty of Heresy."[19] Paul the apostle called it "gangrene," diseased thinking that attacked otherwise healthy tissue (2 Tim. 2:17). From AD 30 onward, each silly lie about God provoked a Bible-based credal confession about Him among His people. Like our immune systems, this was a life-and-death matter. Ben Myers writes,

> It is often said that creeds are political documents, the cunning invention of bishops and councils who are trying to enforce their own understanding of orthodoxy. In the case of the Apostles' Creed, nothing could be further from the truth. It was not part of any deliberate theological strategy. It was a grassroots confession of faith. It was an indigenous form of the ancient church's response to the risen Christ.[20]

One practical use of the creeds was to complement the sermon. If the preacher said something untrue about God or the gospel, reciting the creeds would correct their error. This is why many churches include one of the creeds immediately after the sermon most weeks. No matter what disinformation is being spread in our world and no matter how off the preacher is theologically, we can affirm that we believe the bedrock truth of God.

> No matter what disinformation is being spread, we can affirm that we believe the bedrock truth of God.

Even if your church does not have this practice of regularly reciting the creeds, you can use the creeds in your own prayer and devotional life. They are included in many of the liturgical prayer books. Start with the Apostles' Creed or Nicene Creed. Recite it often, not for the spiritual high, but for your spiritual health. As you confess these truths, remember that your brothers and sisters around the world and throughout time have also made the Good Confession with you.

Jesus taught us to pray, "hallowing" God's name: "Our Father in heaven, hallowed be your name" (Matt. 6:9). Reciting the creeds helps us honor God's name. With all my heart I want to hallow the name of the Father, Son, and Holy Spirit. I want to speak true things about them to myself, to the church, and to the world. Nothing is more destabilizing than God's name being dragged through the mud and lied about. I've done it myself, in my own heart and in my speech, forgetting how good God is. Let's find our stability by taking hold of the beautiful, solid truths set forth in the ancient creeds.

We've talked about the stabilizing power of old prayers, the public reading of Scripture, and the creeds of the early church. There's definitely more about liturgical, sacramental practices that stabilize us. We already covered the healthy stability that can be found in the way we mark time together. We can also seek stability in the regular practice of the Communion meal and baptism and through healthy structures that govern church life and leadership.

But at the end of the day, no amount of liturgy or formality can save us from the onslaught of change. Our true, saving stability is found in Jesus. He is our Refuge, our Rock, our Dwelling Place in all generations (Ps. 90). Together you and I are like living stones being built up as a spiritual house, established securely upon the precious, chosen cornerstone (1 Peter 2:4–6). That building is not for sale. And when the rain falls and the floods come, it will stand.

May your faith—*our* faith—hold fast in these trying times. My prayer for you, friend, is from the letter Jude wrote to the first generation of Christians (vv. 24–25):

> Now to him who is able to keep you from stumbling and to present you blameless before the presence of his glory with great joy, to the only God, our Savior, through Jesus Christ our Lord, be glory, majesty, dominion, and authority, before all time and now and forever. Amen.

VI

LITURGY

THE JOY OF HEAVEN
FOR PEOPLE ON EARTH

What are your associations with liturgy and liturgical churches? Many Christians appreciate worship services that connect them with Jesus. But the use of *liturgy* in those services might feel:

- *Dead,* like a brick in your backpack. Liturgy has no use, it's just heavy, useless dead weight that loads your soul and church with heavy forms of legalism.

- *Boring,* like a wet blanket. You have passion for God that burns bright. Free-form worship stokes that flame higher. Yet for you, liturgy extinguishes it through endless repetition.

- *Strange,* like Grandma's parlor room. Some grandparents have rooms with plastic-covered couches, pictures of the dearly departed, artifacts from their lives, and a list of protocols for how to act when you are in that room. Like your grandma's parlor room, you might associate liturgical services with strange sights, smells, and meanings. The whole environment makes you feel uncomfortable, confused, or obligated. Your whole body screams, "Get me out of here!" You would never invite your friends or neighbors over to hang out in that room with you.

Is it true that liturgy is dead, boring, and strange? Does it load up a life of grace with useless works, nitpicky rules, and funky smells that would turn off the friends and neighbors we want to reach with the gospel? If so, let us be rid of liturgy!

But what if liturgy is not what we always assumed?

What if instead of burdening us, liturgy freed us to live a life of grace?

What if instead of boring us, liturgy, rightly practiced, could usher us into joy?

What if instead of alienating us from the presence of God, liturgical services caught us up into the throne room of God with confidence?

Misconception #1: *Liturgy Is a Dead Religion*
Response: *Liturgy makes us alive.*

Liturgy is any activity of the body that shapes the soul. Liturgy is "the work of the people" that works on the people.[1] It will involve repetition, effort, and discomfort. Yet far from being dead religion, liturgy makes us alive and spiritually awake. In other words, liturgy is meant to be a grace-filled training program that can leave us better prepared to face the trials God allows in our life.

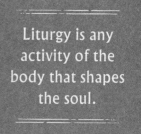

Liturgy is any activity of the body that shapes the soul.

Growing up, I loved basketball. When I reached tenth grade, I was thrilled to join the varsity basketball team. My joy evaporated at the first practice. My first reality check was the conditioning: a whistle would blow, and we went running up and down the court. Another whistle: more running. Whistle, run, whistle, run, whistle, run—sometimes to the garbage can where some would deposit their lunch from earlier in the day. Next came the drills: dribbling, layups, passing, the three-point stance—over and over again, until we got it right. Finally came the plays: learning to run the triangle offense and the full-court press for defense. Then we'd run it again and run it some more—all without an inspiring soundtrack in the background.

Yet I will never forget our first game of the season. We were the clear underdogs. We ran our full-court press at the first opportunity and easily trapped the overconfident point guard. I can still remember seeing the terror on his face as he yelled, "Help!" Though we were scrappier and smaller than our opponents, we could outrun them without getting winded. *So this is what our coach had in mind,* I remember thinking. *Maybe all those drills had a point!* We were alive for the game because we had submitted to the training.

When I look back on the process that shaped our basketball team, I am reminded of the early church. They, too, had their own version of conditioning, drills, and plays that prepared them for victory over the world, the flesh, and the devil. These became known as the "Christian habitus," a battery of liturgies and exercises involving mind, body, memory, and community. Though their world was dangerous and the times unpredictable, their liturgical habits readied ordinary people to stand in Christ no matter what they faced. It was passed on to each generation, whether kids or converts. If you wanted to join the church, the *habitus* was the first thing you learned. And it made the Christian church shine like stars in the universe—it made them alive, not dead. Consider the following example, a fictional account of a typical Christian convert from the early church.

Octavia is a bondservant living in second-century Ephesus. As the eighth-born child (hence the name) to a peasant family, she survives on one meal a day. When her mother dies from the Antonine Plague, Octavia is sold at age thirteen to a wealthy family for domestic labor in exchange for food and lodging. Her already harsh existence becomes more cruel: Octavia now works twelve-hour days, has little family contact, and takes the brunt of the aggression of the household "father." He sexually assaults or beats her without legal consequences.

Yet Octavia is intrigued by Lucia, her fellow slave. She catches Lucia raising her arms into the air, making strange hand movements, or whispering to herself at fixed times throughout the day. Though suffering the same fate as Octavia, Lucia's face radiates with joy. Lucia meets the indignities of bondservitude with a strange confidence normally reserved for noble-born citizens. When Octavia contracts a severe illness, Lucia takes her to a doctor who treats her at no charge. Octavia recovers and joins Lucia for a meal with her "family"—a scandalous mix of slave and free, women and men, Gentiles and Jews, literate and illiterate. Yet they greet each other with a chaste kiss, share their belongings, and all stand together with uplifted arms and confess a strange mystery: *Jesus Christ is Lord, to the glory of God the Father.*

From snatches of conversation at dinner, Octavia learns about the Son of God who became a slave of His own free will, humbling Himself under a Roman crucifixion. The mighty Father who raised Him to life now offers to adopt her as His own child and give His Spirit who brings life. Octavia wants to join this family and confess this mystery. First, Octavia learns the habits: making the sign of the cross in the name of the Father, Son, and Holy Spirit as a spiritual protection, showing hospitality, visiting prisoners, praying the Lord's Prayer, fasting each week, and thanking God in trials, among other habits. It's a lot to learn! She fails often and receives gentle encouragement from her mentors in the community. Gradually Octavia is equipped, along with Lucia, for each trial. The Spirit of Jesus works in the grooves of her new habits to do more than she could imagine possible: forgiving her worst enemies, healing the sick, and drawing joy from another world. Octavia eventually goes into the waters of baptism and emerges as an adopted child in this new family, wearing a robe of white. Weekly worship renews and stabilizes her for the trials ahead.

Within ten years, a local magistrate will press Octavia—upon pain of death—to show allegiance to Caesar through a pinch of incense offered to the emperor. Rather than worship an earthly ruler, with a prayer on her lips she makes the sign of the cross, lifts up her hands, and confesses the mystery: "Jesus Christ is Lord, to the glory of God the Father." Having slipped her bonds of slavery, Octavia enters into that glory, receiving a crown of life and a second white robe.

Early Christians like Octavia used gospel liturgy to train for trials and emerge victorious from them. The repetition and habits practiced "off the spot" gave them the freedom to obey Christ when they were put "on the spot." The same was true of Christ Himself.

Consider Jesus under extreme stress and trial: He applies old prayers to new challenges. In the garden of Gethsemane, Jesus is hours away from trial, scourging, and ultimate sacrifice on the cross. Notice what He prays: "My Father, if it be possible, let this cup pass from me; nevertheless, not as I will, but as you will" (Matt. 26:39). Can you hear the echoes of the prayer He taught His disciples to pray? *Our Father ... deliver us from evil ... your will be done.* He prays it again, and then a third time, using the same words: *My Father ... your will be done* (Matt. 26:42, 44). The Lord's Prayer is in His memory. He needs it. He prays it again and again. Even on the cross, we can hear a final echo of *Our Father ... forgive us as we forgive those who sin against us*: "Father, forgive them, for they know not what they do" (Luke 23:34). Jesus has run His drills, He's done His reps, and He is ready for His fight.

Are we ready for ours? Contemporary Christians could take a page from Jesus' playbook. Many people in the pews are struggling in their prayer life. With biblical illiteracy on the rise, fewer are holding to basic theological orthodoxy. Even more concerning are the rising numbers of children raised in Christian homes

who abandon their faith in high school or college. Even for th
who stay, the rates of mental health struggles, including depres-
sion and anxiety, continue to climb.

Are our non-liturgical Christian practices really making us
alive for the moment?

We stand in need of life-giving
rituals that can impart healing
for the soul, training in prayer,
and good gospel theology, all in
the powerful presence of Jesus
Christ. In other words, liturgy
isn't just a brick in the backpack.
Christian liturgy, in the power
of the Holy Spirit, is a *habitus*
for our day. Gospel-filled liturgy
strengthens the heart, enlivens

> We stand in need of life-giving rituals that can impart healing for the soul, training in prayer, and good gospel theology, all in the powerful presence of Jesus Christ.

the will, and exercises the soul. Gospel liturgy makes us vigorous
and strong for faithful obedience to Jesus.

During the Eastertide season at Immanuel, we end our services
with something called "the Kenyan Blessing." Along with the
pastor, the whole congregation stands to their feet and extends
their hands toward a visible cross as they say,

Officiant: All our problems of this life on earth,

People: We send to the cross of Christ!

Officiant: All the difficulties of our circumstances,

People: We send to the cross of Christ!

Officiant: All the devil's work from his temporary power,

People: We send to the cross of Christ![2]

There's a sense of defiant joy and relief as we place our sicknesses, conflicts, injustices, curses, or any number of problems under the authority of the cross of Christ. This also serves as an exercise we take into the rest of the week, where the problems, difficulties, and attacks of the evil one continue to test our faith. The blessing ends with everyone lifting their hands toward heaven, as they conclude,

Officiant: All our hopes for wholeness and eternal life,

People: We set on the Risen Christ!

Officiant: May Christ the sun of righteousness, shine on you and scatter the darkness before your path. And may the blessing of God Almighty, the Father, Son, and Holy Spirit, be among you and remain with you always. Amen![3]

Misconception #2: *Liturgy Is Boring*
Response: *Liturgy is joy.*

Some celebrations are so joyful that liturgy erupts all by itself.

I risk alienating some readers by confessing that I am a Chicago Cubs fan. For 108 years the Cubs went without winning a World Series, and legend has it that this was the result of a Billy Goat curse (I leave the research to you, dear reader). Generations of fans lived and died without seeing the Cubbies—known as "the Lovable Losers"—take the World Championship for faithful fans.

So when the Cubs won the World Series in game seven against the Cleveland Indians in November 2016, the north side of Chicago went berserk. At the time my family rented an apartment not far from Wrigley Field. After the victory was secured, horns and cheers sounded outside our window. I couldn't stay inside, so I put on my running shoes and made a pilgrimage to the Friendly Confines along with tens of thousands of others. Perfect strangers high-fived, hugged, cried, and danced in the streets. With so much joy, we reached for the ultimate liturgical action known to every Cubs fan: the song "Go, Cubs, Go," a hokey anthem-turned-classic by Steve Goodman.

Fans learn to sing this song after every victory, especially at Wrigley Field. You are supposed to sway back and forth while you sing (at least that's how I received the tradition). "Go, Cubs, Go" is nothing less than a liturgical practice that teaches and expresses joy in the Cubs, win or lose. So after the World Series triumph, this liturgy was the best way for us to channel the joy erupting from our hearts.

Have you ever participated in a joy-filled wedding? Chances are that liturgy was involved somehow. Traditionally, the liturgical movement begins far in advance with a proposal ("Will you marry me?" on bended knee), followed by the father of the bride walking his daughter down the aisle, parting a sea of loved ones who stand in awe of her beauty.

The pastor asks pointed liturgical questions: "Will you have this woman to be your wife? . . . Will you love her, honor her, comfort and keep her, in sickness and in health, and forsaking all others, be faithful to her as long as you both shall live?" We all know the correct liturgical response: "I do."[4] Vows are taken, rings are exchanged, a kiss-to-end-all-kisses, on the mouth, is kissed, a newly married couple is introduced. Cheers erupt.

But the wedding liturgy doesn't end there. Liturgy moves us through to the end: a dance for the father of the bride and his daughter, the same for the mother of the groom and her son, followed by feasting, dancing, and toasts and roasts to the happy couple.

Whatever the celebration, liturgy does not compete with joy. In most cases, liturgy clarifies the joy. Liturgy helps us channel our joy. Joy and liturgy go together like a bride and groom.

Did you know that each Sunday is like a joyful wedding feast?

Liturgy helps us channel our joy.

That is how many of the first pastors of the church thought of it: our beloved groom Jesus Christ gave His life to be united with His bride, the church. He loves us with a love stronger than death. His blood covers our offenses and makes us worthy to stand in a pure wedding dress, without spot or wrinkle, in great splendor. As we approach Him each Sunday, our Groom sings over us, speaks His love over us, and is quite ready to embrace us in love.[5]

Each line of the liturgy, every time we say "Amen," every full-throated "Alleluia! Alleluia!" during Easter, and every time we lift the chalice and drink the new wine of His covenant comprises our joyful "I do."

I acknowledge that not every liturgical service is filled with joy. It should be! Similarly, not every non-liturgical service is filled with joy. In both cases, *liturgy itself is not the problem.* Churches and services without joy need the presence of the Holy Spirit. They need pastors whose souls have been refreshed and have had some training in leading the liturgy in a heartfelt way. They need congregations ready to follow and participate with whole hearts.

Liturgical churches in the global south (including Africa, Asia, and South America) model joyful participation well. They lead the liturgy with passion, with leaders and congregants alike even dancing during songs, as they bring forward their gifts to the altar, and in seasons of the church that call for joy.

One of the most difficult blocks to joy in liturgy is how unfamiliar it is. Let's discuss that next.

Misconception #3: *Liturgy Is Strange*
Response: *Liturgy is a cultural bridge, a citizenship class for heaven, strange on purpose.*

I have a friend with a huge heart for evangelism. He's concerned that liturgy is a stumbling block for the unchurched because it is so strange. In his message to me, he wrote, "Unbelievers without liturgical backgrounds feel alienated from liturgical church services. It's like requiring a secret handshake when you walk into the living room. The whole experience of unfamiliar words and gestures can leave first-time participants feeling like outsiders."

This common concern contains some truth. Consider the following strange elements of a worship service at the church I lead (Immanuel Anglican Church in Chicago):

- I wear a white robe. Few people in Chicago, especially grown men, wear a white robe in public. What's more, a cloth hangs around my neck that is color-coded to the liturgical season we are in.

- Before the gospel passage is read aloud, a minister picks up a large gospel book, holds it aloft, and processes around while the congregation sings the word "Alleluia" over and over again. The singing and the processing happen again after the reading is over.

- People worship with their bodies. They make the sign of the cross (sometimes over their *lips!*), kneel, bow, stand, raise up their hands, and drink from a common cup.

- We burn incense on "Feast Days" so that the aroma and smoke fill the sanctuary.

- I engage in a formal call-and-response with the congregation. We talk to each other, like actors in a drama, using lines from Scripture. Here's an example:

Pastor: The Lord be with you.

People: And also with you.

Pastor: Lift up your hearts! *(I raise my hands)*

People: We lift them up to the Lord! *(They raise their hands)*

Pastor: Let us give thanks to the Lord our God.

People: It is right to give Him thanks and praise.

In our modern world, who does this? Who talks like this? Why wouldn't we use more casual, off-the-cuff, less formal language? And what purpose is there in strange sights, funny clothes, and processions? No wonder people leave confused.

Of all the charges against liturgy that could be made, this one might land. Liturgy is strange—it's strange on purpose. Liturgy trains us for citizenship in our true home and city, the New Jerusalem. We are learning the language and customs in advance. It

Liturgy is strange—it's strange on purpose.

feels awkward at first, but over time it enculturates us to the city where we will live forever.

Have you ever visited a foreign country and found it difficult to understand the local customs, language, and food? The funky smells and foreign sounds make us homesick. After a trip abroad, we might want to sleep in our own beds and eat our favorite comfort foods. Yet if we can persist in learning local customs, a whole world opens up to us that was inaccessible otherwise. We are never the same afterward.

Take my friend Mary. She grew up in China. Yet due to state-led persecution of her Christian parents, she found herself in America at age twelve. The first surprise for her was how much personal space people had, both in conversation and in yard space. In China, people speak, live, and exist in close quarters. On top of that, Americans hugged a lot. Mary found that disorienting; hugging is not common in China except with family. Compared with Chinese culture, Americans are hugely into sports, whether they're playing or watching. With the help of the Lord and her host family, Mary learned the English language from knowing very little all the way to fluency. Day by day, Mary grew to love the once-strange country, both its people and customs. Last I heard, Mary placed first in her fantasy football league, beating out her husband and all his friends!

Of all the places you or I could travel, heaven itself might be the strangest. The throne room of God is a distinct place with unique, stunning, even terrifying features. Each person given access is never the same. When Isaiah received a vision of God's throne room (Isa. 6:1–13), he saw the Lord exalted and clothed in splendor. Otherworldly creatures with six wings made gestures and sang a liturgical song about God's holiness. If this wasn't unnerving enough, the sound of God's voice thundered, causing an earthquake beneath Isaiah's feet as the room filled with smoke.

Heaven's strangeness shook Isaiah's body. It shook Isaiah's soul. This was not a user-friendly worship experience that left him ready to fill out a connection card. Yet enough of it got through: he knew that his unclean lips and his unclean life needed cleaning, that without help he was undone. He looked on God and was about to die.

More strange liturgy followed. The seraphim flew to Isaiah with a burning coal and kissed his mouth with it. Atonement was made.

The liturgy ended with a call-and-response: the Lord asked, "Whom shall I send? And who will go with me?" Isaiah responded with a vow of willing service: "Here am I; send me." Isaiah left the vision and went into the world ready to fulfill his calling.

If a door to heaven opened before you, would you walk through it? Would you visit this strange and wonderful place, this terrifying realm? If so, what do you imagine you would see? How might it change you?

This happened to a man named John. John was exiled for his commitment to Jesus and the gospel. At one point, he had a vision (whether dreaming or awake, I do not know) that showed him a door opened to heaven. A trumpet-like voice invited him to walk through it. As he followed the voice through the door, John found himself before God's throne. Craning his neck upward to take in the massive sight, John saw God the Father clothed in the beauties of the earth, including jasper, carnelian, and an emerald-hued rainbow. John noticed that God's throne thundered with power yet towered over a calm and clear body of water. It's the kind of vision that leaves a person falling on his face in awe.

John then saw a pageant of earthly and heavenly creatures humble themselves before God. Angels, animals, and authorities began a liturgy, each playing their role. "Holy, holy, holy is the Lord God Almighty, who was and is and is to come!" cried the heavenly creatures (Rev. 4:8). The earthly leaders took their cue and cried out in response: "Worthy are you, our Lord and God, to receive glory and honor and power!" while lying prostrate on heaven's floor. You and I are accustomed to the created order in conflict—divided over scarce resources, fighting and killing one another. Yet this diverse gathering was united by the worthiness of God. No one competed with God for attention. No one denigrated the contributions of the others. They simply entered into a liturgy of praise together, harmonizing to God's holiness.

There's more to the vision. If you want to read the rest of John's testimony and the strange, beautiful liturgies that he witnessed, you can find it in the book of Revelation.

I'll ask a second time: If a door to heaven opened to you, and a voice invited you to "Come up here," would you follow the voice and walk through that door? Might you, dare you, enter the liturgy of heaven?

The door is open, my friend. The door to heaven's glory and heaven's liturgy has been opened to you by the blood of Jesus. Enter it. Follow the voice to the throne. Join the liturgical assembly, bow down, and rejoice.

In the words of the author of Hebrews, writing a pastoral encouragement to a suffering flock: "Let us then with confidence draw near to the throne of grace, that we may receive mercy and find grace to help in time of need" (Heb. 4:16). That's the throne room he's talking about—the one in heaven, where we can sing, confess, and bow down before God along with all His heavenly hosts. Later in his letter, the same pastor said this:

> You have come to Mount Zion and to the city of the living God, the heavenly Jerusalem, and to innumerable angels in festal gathering, and to the assembly of the firstborn who are enrolled in heaven, and to God, the judge of all, and to the spirits of the righteous made perfect, and to Jesus, the mediator of a new covenant, and to the sprinkled blood that speaks a better word than the blood of Abel. (Heb. 12:22–24)

Notice the writer says *you have come*—not *you will go there one day*. You *have* come. The assembly around the throne includes you. If you are in Christ, your life is hidden with Christ in God. Your truest self is not found anywhere on this earth.

Sometimes I remind our congregation that we can visualize our gathered worship as being joined with the worship of heaven—

with angels all around us, dearly departed saints, the thunder and the emeralds, the sea of glass, and the Lamb who was slain. We might be a bunch of stragglers and strugglers. Yet "Christ's heavenly liturgy [is placed] squarely in the midst of the liturgical gathering of the humble, suffering community."[6] The Holy Spirit lifts us up to that assembly each time we gather in the name of Jesus. As we come to the Eucharist, the minister always says, "Lift up

> If you are in Christ, your life is hidden with Christ in God. Your truest self is not found anywhere on this earth.

your hearts" and the congregation responds, "We lift them up to the Lord." And there we go—through the door, to the throne, up where we belong.

Each time we gather to worship, we set our minds on things above. We learn the customs of things above. We involve our bodies in things above. We come to the throne of grace with confidence, bold enough to praise, humble enough to bow. We let God shake us like Isaiah and invite us up like John. If liturgy is strange, it should be strange on purpose.

Could there be anything more powerful for a non-believer to encounter than the living God in a worship service? One historian notes that the number one cause for conversions in the early church was deliverance from demonic oppression in the worship service.[7] In the context of throne-room worship, liturgical and Spirit-filled, the power of God came near and triumphed over all other powers. In the words of Edith Humphrey, "Worship . . . may cause an unbeliever's heart to be unveiled, so that he or she will join in the worship and cry, 'God is really among you.'"[8]

A Word to Pastors and Leaders

Fellow pastors and worship leaders, let's not confuse strange with meaningless. Our liturgical actions, words, and decisions should be purposeful and intentional. We can and should translate them for the unchurched whenever possible. This is both faithful shepherding and evangelistic. We can have a service with distinct Christian elements and be welcoming at the same time.

This involves explaining what the customs are and why we do them. In our church, we give each visitor a "Field Guide to Sunday Worship" so they know what each part of the service means. We also take time in the worship service, in our membership retreat, and our confirmation class to explain what is happening in worship.

Do I have to join a "liturgical" church to benefit from liturgy?

No! Liturgy is for all Christians and all churches, and there's no "one size fits all" approach to incorporating it in worship and prayer. No matter your church's denomination, culture, style of music, or tradition, there are likely liturgical elements that you can appreciate. For instance, even if your church celebrates Communion only once a month or quarter, you can prepare for that Sunday with a day of fasting and repentance. Or if you long for more liturgy in your personal devotional life, you might purchase a *Book of Common Prayer* and pray through the Daily Office in the morning and evenings. Take note of elements in your church's worship service that repeat themselves, and ask the Holy Spirit to use this repetition to shape you to love God and your neighbor with greater depth.

It might be time to rethink our assumptions about liturgy.

Rather than being a brick in the backpack that weighs us down, liturgy can be a gospel habit that makes us alive.

Rather than being a wet blanket that kills joy, Spirit-filled liturgy can be a wedding banquet that intensifies our joy.

Rather than being like Grandma's parlor room, liturgy from the beginning was intended to take us and our unchurched friends before the Father's throne room.

Good liturgy isn't dead, boring, or strange. It may have become that, but from the beginning it was not so.

VII

PASSING THE PEACE

CHRISTIAN UNITY IN A DIVIDED WORLD

Peace. Don't you long for it? We need peace in our homes, peace in our families, peace in our churches, peace in our towns and cities and countries. We still need peace on earth and goodwill toward men and women.

When I feel peace, so much feels possible: creative work, playing, praying, building, taking good risks, even sleeping. All the energy so often spent on worrying or fighting can be finally invested in the work of justice and worship and raising kids.

The peace of God in Christ is the source of all peace in this life. And from it, we can enjoy peace with His people. That is where liturgy and the sacramental life come in: by God's grace, these gifts can shape us to be people of peace. Even in a time of division and polarization, we can practice it together, imperfectly and provocatively.

A Liturgy of Blood and Blame

The ancient world was brutal. The Colosseum, along with the amphitheaters across the Roman Empire, symbolized this brutality. Event organizers would draw in spectators by the tens of thousands to watch prisoners and enemies of the state cower before wild beasts and trained gladiators.

The appeal for the common citizen was clear: they got to watch bad people suffer public humiliation and death. Despicable human beings, threats to them and their families and the common good, got their just deserts. The people got to watch the boar bury its tusks inside the wrongdoers' bellies. No matter how much the criminals protested, they would not escape the arena alive. What a thrill! Not only that, spectators were safely tucked away in the crowds, anonymous and good participating citizens. Onlookers were not responsible for the killings and never got their hands bloodied, per se. Citizens were just doing their part, cheering on the demise of the vile and heinous, feeling superior and being entertained in the process.

This all worked for the political leaders and cultural gatekeepers as well. For starters, an entertained populace is a happy one. Happy spectators are, by definition, passive supporters, less likely to challenge the status quo of the power structure. What's more, by making a violent spectacle of political prisoners, leaders were forming their people to accept, even to love, the violent order of which they were a part. And let's be honest, every politician loves a crowd.[1]

Coliseum killings were a liturgy of blood and blame. They shocked with schadenfreude, that dark-chocolate pleasure of watching an enemy suffer misfortune. No wonder the ancient world was so tribalized and violent; violence was habituated until it was all the people knew.

The Psychological Coliseum

Now the Roman Colosseum has crumbled, and in contemporary culture we have erected our own psychological coliseum. The technology is different—it's an arena built with phones instead of stones—but the spiritual condition is the same. We love to watch the baddies suffer. The thrill of the kill is too much to resist, and it brings us together almost every day.

My kids alerted me to a genre of internet videos known as "instant karma." The idea is this: someone decides to be a jerk to someone else, and it backfires. For instance, a little girl torments a cat and gets scratched, or an aggressive driver pulls an illegal move and is instantly pulled over by an undercover cop, or a cyclist makes an impolite gesture and crashes immediately after. Instant karma videos are mostly lighthearted, home video versions of delicious poetic justice. I confess they are also slightly addicting.

Instant karma is even more fun and engrossing when you can watch it happen in real time on social media and cheer it on in the privacy of your personal space. In the words of one anonymous-yet-popular Twitter handle: "Each day on twitter there is one main character. The goal is to never be it."[2] Whatever the outlet, be it online or cable news, there is usually someone, a main character if you will, who has transgressed a moral boundary deemed unacceptable by the group. Maybe the target is a public figure who snaps at a lawmaker at the end of a hearing, or a private citizen in one of the worst moments of his or her life, or a late-night alcohol-fueled rant that is later deleted—only too late.[3]

How often have we looked on, feeling at once shocked and superior, as the offending main character is dragged into the center of internet scorn, their sins confessed, their reputations ruined, their job lost, their career derailed? And why not? Maybe they are, after all, a threat to society, and social media was the only way for these pariahs to get their well-deserved comeuppance.[4] But what do *we* deserve, we who cheer on their demise? And what kind of person do we become as we passively scroll and watch and repost? What are we teaching our hearts to love? What kind of mercy would we want on the day when, God forbid, *we* become the main character?

> We cannot take our unity in Christ for granted— unity in Christ has to be exercised.

You cannot participate in amphitheater violence without being formed by the experience. We can see the impact in our churches, as we take our formation during the week into the holy assembly: small differences becoming huge rifts, political tribes splitting congregations, the people of God assuming the worst of one another, rumors, racism, revenge, motive-judging, psychoanalyzing, and the spiritual pain of passive betrayal. We cannot take our unity in Christ for granted—unity in Christ has to be exercised.

Kissing Christians

Have you ever read the words "Greet one another with a holy kiss" in the Bible, and thought, "Paul and Peter must have been speaking metaphorically; surely they weren't instructing us to kiss each other on the lips!" Or maybe there was a special someone in your local church with whom you secretly wished to practice this Bible verse. Best of luck on that one.

For us, kissing carries connotations of romantic or family bonds, such as a husband kissing his wife or a mother kissing her son. In the Roman Empire, kissing surely included those relationships, but it could also communicate status. If you observed two people kissing in public, the message was likely this: "We are equals, comrades, of the same social ranking." In a culture as stratified and hierarchical as any in history, citizens only offered a kiss to those on their level.[5] Anything else was a scandal—not of a sexual nature, but a societal one.

The Christian message attracted people up and down the social ladder. The structures outside the church pulled them apart. And surely sin and cultural differences made unity difficult. Yet the gospel declared them no less than family members, reconciled through the blood of Jesus and having equal standing in the sight of God.

Enter the holy kiss, the "kiss of peace." In the early worship services, the Bible teaching would lead into a time of confession:

confession of the Christian creed, confessing sins, and finally confessing the peace of Christ to one another through a kiss.[6] Before anyone could join in the intercessory prayers or approach the Communion table to partake in the meal of Jesus, they had to practice peacemaking. This was a moment to reconcile any broken relationships, pardon any known grievances, and declare their equal standing through a holy kiss. Men with men, women with women. The kiss said, in effect, "I wish for your well-being, that though the world outside pits us against each other, counting me as more important than you, in Christ we are one, though we may not feel this way on the inside."

Surely this was an awkward part of the liturgy. Imagine it: centurions kissing peasants, freeborn citizens kissing bondservants, Jews kissing Gentiles, merchants kissing stone masons, sinners kissing sinners. It was not a free-for-all, but a carefully monitored, prayerful, and sober family moment for God's people. It's so much more than the exchange of a kiss: sins are confessed, forgiveness is sought, misunderstandings overcome, status games abandoned. If someone in the assembly had offended you, there was no way around getting close enough to see the whites of their eyes, where the fears and tears and humanity was. It was close, direct, and humble, which is the only way reconciliation really happens.

One church historian captures how important this was for the early church, which was both messy and multicultural:

> This . . . (non-homogeneous) group of people had to learn to live together. This was not easy. They missed each other's cultural cues, and they offended each other . . . They viewed their common life as a miracle, but they were on a journey in

which miscues and misunderstandings were inevitable. So when they assembled for their weekly services in which they prayed and shared in the Lord's Supper, in the kiss of peace they celebrated their unity in Christ and asked forgiveness for their sins that hurt each other.[7]

The reason we offer a handshake, a hug, or even a chaste kiss as part of our liturgy is to reenact the unity we have in Christ. If we are unwilling to do this, we are not ready for the feast of our Lord. Jesus Himself instructed us about this when He said: "So if you are offering your gift at the altar and there remember that your brother has something against you, leave your gift there before the altar and go. First be reconciled to your brother, and then come and offer your gift" (Matt. 5:23–24).

In the words of Cyprian, the great pastor of the persecuted Christians in Carthage: "God does not accept the sacrifice of one who is in dispute, and sends him back from the altar, ordering him first to be reconciled to his brother ... The greater sacrifice to God is our peace and brotherly agreement, as a people unified in the unity of the Father and the Son and the Holy Spirit."[8]

Our greeting to our fellow Christians is meant to be much more than "Say hello to your neighbor." The deeper significance of this moment is to say, "As I am forgiven, I forgive you; please forgive me. I also accept you as my brother or sister in Christ; we are not stratified but equals. Let's go to the table of Jesus together and receive mercy together, as beggars and as brothers and sisters."

This part of the worship service reminds me of the novel-turned-movie *Babette's Feast.* Babette is a French-trained chef who works in a strict Danish household. The small village is divided over old hurts and resentments. The sisters she works for have long-forgotten romances that never worked out.

One day Babette wins 10,000 francs in the lottery and becomes fantastically wealthy. Babette could escape the joyless work environment and pursue her art in France; that's what everyone around her expects her to do. Instead, she spends every last franc on a singular, sumptuous feast. The catch is that it's not just for the sisters she works for but for everyone they've fallen out with, even their former suitors.

As everyone takes their seats in awkward silence, they sip on the turtle soup, munch on endive salad, and grunt in delight at the quail in puff-pastry shells. As the guests make furtive eye contact, the sacrificial grace of Babette's meal starts melting their icy resentments. Out of enemies, a community is born.[9]

The truth is that the personal sacrifice of Jesus is what makes our unity possible. Without Jesus pouring out His blood, there would be no forgiveness of sins. Without Jesus' physical body being broken, the body of Christ could never heal from its divisions. When we say, "May the peace of Christ be with you" to someone who hurt us, we confess this mystery. When we eat the bread or drink the cup at the Lord's Table, we proclaim this mystery.

> The personal sacrifice of Jesus is what makes our unity possible.

Where can our friends and neighbors go after they have been canceled, rejected, and judged? Could there be a table of grace, a community of peace, placed right in the heart of a graceless and condemning land of instant karma?

Bono, the lead singer and front man for the band U2, expresses his own personal longing for this:

> You see, at the center of all religions is the idea of Karma. You know, what you put out comes back to you: an eye for an eye, a tooth for a tooth, or in physics—in physical laws—every action is met by an equal or an opposite one. It's clear to me that Karma is at the very heart of the Universe. I'm absolutely sure of it. And yet, along comes this idea called Grace to upend all that "As you reap, so you will sow" stuff. Grace defies reason and logic. Love interrupts, if you like, the consequences of your actions, which in my case is very good news indeed, because I've done a lot of stupid stuff. . . .
>
> But I'd be in big trouble if Karma was going to finally be my judge. . . . It doesn't excuse my mistakes, but I'm holding out for Grace. I'm holding out that Jesus took my sins onto the Cross, because I know who I am, and I hope I don't have to depend on my own religiosity.[10]

If instant karma is all we have, we will be quite eager to hide our sins and expose everyone else's. But if we truly have the grace of our Lord, we will be free to reverse this dynamic, freely confessing our own sins and covering the sins of others.

No Justice, No Peace

You might be thinking: "Aaron, you're being sentimental and naïve. Forgiving Christians have, by this logic, allowed abusive

121

and narcissistic people to avoid responsibility for their sins and continue preying on the weak. Also, some wounds and conflicts take more than some liturgical actions to resolve. If there's no justice, there's no peace."

Those objections are legitimate. Human beings are complex; human conflicts are even more complex; and there's no simple, easy, one-size-fits-all approach to resolving them. Unity involves the slow and patient work of godly church discipline; integrating our discipleship with our emotions, relationships, and cultural awareness; learning to practice the fruit of the Spirit; holding offenders responsible for their actions, and in many cases involving mediators, counselors, pastors, and even law enforcement to help resolve long-standing grievances. Liturgy is part of a larger picture of faithful pastoral care. The peace of Christ is a gift, though it takes time and maturity to practice it together.[11]

Not every person will be willing to repent of his or her part in a conflict. That was true in Jesus' day and persists even now. Yet for those who are willing, the church's greatest gift to them is a place at the table, where swords are beaten into plowshares and spears into pruning hooks (Isa. 2:3–4).

In Michael Card's song "Come to the Table," he captures the relief available to all who, upon offering and receiving forgiveness, approach the Eucharist with glad and humble hearts: "If you'll come to the table, you'll feel in your heart the greatest forgiveness, the greatest release."[12]

Kissing in the Coliseum

By AD 203, the Christian gospel had taken root near Carthage, a city in Roman Africa just south of the Tyrrhenian Sea. Unfortunately, the local government saw this small local church as a threat to its well-being and imprisoned at least six of its members.[13] Eventually these young men and women were sold on the cheap to the local government to die in the Carthage amphitheater as entertainment for the masses and as food for the wild beasts.

After weeks of spiritual preparation in jail, this small group of disciples marched with confidence into the jeering mob. They were not only willing to die; they were determined to preach the gospel with their bodies in the process of death. By refusing both the costumes of the Greek gods and the opportunity to pay homage to the emperor, they provoked the crowd to a frothing rage. There was no going back: today they would be the main characters of Carthage.

A leopard and a female cow went to work on the Christians, in turns tossing, piercing, and stunning their bodies. How long this took, we do not know. Yet we do know the provocative unity shown at the end. Historian Alan Krieder captures the moment:

> At the very end, after most of the Christians had been seriously wounded by the animals, the crowd's interest was still lively, for they asked that all Christians be brought to a central spot where they could see clearly as the gladiator's sword finished them off. They saw the executions; but they also saw the Christians muster the strength of body and will to stand up, gather themselves as a group in the specified spot, and give a final

embodied witness. These disparate people, women and men, slave and free, poor and advantaged, "kissed each other so that they might bring their martyrdom to completion with the kiss of peace." Exhausted and in pain though they were, in extremis the prisoners did reflexively, virtually on autopilot, what they had been habituated to do in their services of worship—*they exchanged the kiss of peace, embodying a love that transcended social barriers.*[14]

In the epicenter of coliseum violence, the Christians demonstrated the peace of Christ. By showing the world the gift of reconciliation, won by the blood of Christ, they invited all of Carthage to know this mystery. We know from the historical record that their jailer, Puden, converted that very day. Others in the crowd began to question their own violent values and beliefs.

When I consider their example, I am sobered and inspired. I want to be like these Carthagian Christians, united across social classes, forgiving, courageous. I feel convicted that far too often I have been more like the Colosseum crowds: scrolling through social media for the next fight, cheering on the demise of the next villain, assuming the worst of people I don't understand, and growing addicted to feeling offended and morally superior. Maybe you're in the same boat. We could sure use that grace Bono was talking about.

What if we reversed the dynamic, and instead of the violence of our world infecting our churches, the peace of Christ began to infect our world? It could start with those awkward "I'm sorry, would you forgive me?" moments before Communion. It could begin with common confessions of sin—that we have not done what we ought to have but have done what we were not supposed to do. It could begin with saying, "May the peace of the Lord be always with you" and meaning it. It could start with our own version of *Babette's Feast*, maybe a barbeque after church with people outside our socioeconomic circle with whom we go to church.

It could start with responding to a social media controversy with an offline redemptive conversation where understanding is shared and misconceptions are overcome rather than exacerbated.

If you have been deeply hurt by another Christian, maybe this feels impossible and foolish. Everything in you may want to lash out, power up, and balance the scale of justice once and for all. Violence—in what-

> Though the way of peace feels weak and humble, it is actually stronger than the way of violence.

ever form it takes—just seems like the only real way toward lasting peace. Given what you have endured, it makes sense that you would have this perspective. Yet please hear me out. Though the way of peace feels weak and humble, it is actually stronger than the way of violence. In the words of one pastor:

> The way of Jesus is more stern and splendid, more rock-like and lasting, more beautiful than the Temple stones of old Jerusalem. Christ's temple is always built on the knees—in humbled prayer, hand-to-foot washings, reconciliations with tears—and framed-out with cross beams, mortared in blood, often from hearts pierced by betrayal and abandonment. His

Temple-Body is raised up in cruciform glory. That is how it becomes unshakable.[15]

With each act of peace, that Temple is built up. And when all the coliseums of this world have crumbled, God's Temple will stand forever.

(But in the meantime, it's probably best not to go around kissing people at church.)

VIII

THE PRAYERS OF THE PEOPLE

BONFIRE OF THE ANXIETIES

A good bonfire is a sight to behold. The best setting for a bonfire is a cold, dark night with plenty of fuel to burn. The warmth and dazzle of a strong flame against a dark sky will entertain for hours. What's more, you can use it as an excuse to clean out your shed, home, or property of anything combustible. Most everyone has something to contribute: scraps of wood, fallen leaves, torn clothes, or an old textbook from a class they hated. I am told that in Texas, a notorious bonfire might consume felled oak trees and run on jet fuel![1] In rural Ohio we would use old raspberry canes from the garden to keep the fire lit. In urban Chicago, we got through the pandemic with backyard firepits where friends and family could gather outside.

Beyond the entertainment value, bonfires are a matter of economic efficiency. People collect their unwanted clutter and debris into a common pile, set it ablaze, and thereby release its kinetic energy for its warmth, beauty, and power to cook food.

Bonfire of the Anxieties

What if the church could provide a space for us to collect the debris of our anxieties, the rotting wood of our hardships, the kindling of our passions, the jet fuel of our anger, and the felled logs of our hope for God's kingdom to come, and set it all ablaze in prayer together? What if there were a place for our groanings, sufferings, expectations, and longing for renewal to be cast into a bonfire of prayer? The best setting for this is the world we live in: a cold, dark night with plenty of fuel to burn.

Maybe there, in that bonfire of prayer, is where the church's renewal will begin: in collective weakness, as the kinetic energy of our fears and failures are released in passionate, united prayer to the Father, Son, and Holy Spirit. Things cannot stay the same when that happens.

> Christians need a sustainable, biblically grounded, time-tested way to keep the fires of prayer going week by week, year by year.

Yet Christians also need a sustainable, biblically grounded, time-tested way to keep the fires of prayer going week by week, year by year. Just as a literal fire has both kindling and logs, so the church at prayer needs both personal passion and theological ballast.

What's more, we need a way to involve our bodies in the process, lifting up holy hands, kneeling in contrition, and engaging all of our senses in prayer. This might be the most alien and scary part of ancient Christian prayer. Yet as we'll see, this is a deeply biblical and Christ-centered way to approach the throne of grace.

The ancient church modeled all embodied prayer for us. For all her faults, the ancient church was not an anxious church. She was a church at prayer, a church on fire. We will explore three ways we can keep the fires of collective prayer burning: through confession, collective prayers, and the prayers of the people, an old form of intercession.

Before we go too far back into history, we'll share in a story from the more recent past.

The Moravian Pentecost

One of the most stirring accounts of the church at prayer is from the Moravian Church, one of the first Protestant movements. After years of persecution, in 1722 a group of young Christians from Moravia (the modern-day Czech Republic) found shelter on a plot of land owned by Count Zinzendorf. Zinzendorf was a Christian landowner with a heart to serve the marginalized. No longer nomads, believers settled into a small town they called Herrnhut ("The Lord's watchful care").

As often happens in churches, what began peaceably devolved into factions and fighting. As each camp dug in their heels on matters of secondary importance, their love of God and neighbor grew cold. Rather than passively watch the community fracture,

Zinzendorf went house to house with an open Bible. He entreated each family to return to the basics of following Jesus: love of God and love of neighbor, lived out together in common prayer, worship, and mission.

In time, every single faction agreed to return to the basics of Christian discipleship. On August 13, 1727, the residents of Herrnhut gathered for a worship service, complete with preaching from the Scriptures, Communion, and a public commitment to unity.

Then something surprising happened. During the worship service, the leaders made space for people to confess their sins. How this happened is lost to history: whether out loud or silently, in a large group or small huddles. One way or another, the toxic buildup of resentment, pride, backbiting, and religious idolatry was set to a common flame. Everyone had debris of the soul to add to the burn pile, which grew hotter and higher with each confession.

Without warning, the presence of God overwhelmed the confessing congregation. Twenty-seven years later, Count Zinzendorf recounted it as if it were yesterday:

> We needed to come to the communion with a sense of the loving nearness of the Savior . . . because on this day twenty-seven years ago the Congregation of Herrnhut, assembled for communion . . . were all dissatisfied with themselves. They had quit judging each other because they had become convinced, each one, of his lack of worth in the sight of God and each felt himself at this communion to be in view of the noble countenance of the Saviour.[2]

As they left the church service around noon, they were nearly speechless, "hardly knowing whether they belonged to earth or had already gone to heaven."[3] It seems the dead weight of unconfessed sin was lifted from Herrnhut, and in its place, a burning holy fire. This event became known as the "Moravian Pentecost," and it sparked a hundred-year streak of unbroken prayer, which in turn fueled frontier missions to every continent on the earth.[4]

Don't you long for God to do it again?

A Place for Confession

One of the advantages of liturgy is a consistent space in prayer and worship for people to unburden their souls in confession. Most of the time this unburdening will not be as dramatic as the Moravian Pentecost. We can entrust that to the Lord. Personally, I would take a healthy, sustainable, slow-burn spiritual life over a boom-and-bust cycle of revival and relapse any day.

The driving force behind confession of sin is to maintain an upright relationship with a holy God and with His people. Confession helps us move past pretense into a dynamic, healthy encounter with Jesus Christ. As I study the original Pentecost in Acts 2 and the events to follow, one thing becomes clear: the Holy Spirit has no appetite for religious pretense. In the assembly of worship, people were cut to the heart (Acts 2:37), called to repent (Acts 2:38; 3:19), publicly exposed for lying (Acts 5:1–11), and called on the carpet for being stiff-necked and killing God's messengers (Acts 7:51–53).

Even in the church's infancy, we see the Lord exposing sin, not to shame people but to heal them. Isn't this just a bit refreshing?

The Lord has no appetite for pretending or playing silly religious games. You probably don't, either. Have you ever tried relating on a deep level with people who are always trying to cover over their weaknesses? It's exhausting! But once sin and dysfunction are exposed, the Lord can heal, redeem, and change a life or a community, like the Moravians. "Confess your sins to one another, and pray for one another, that you may be healed," said the brother of Jesus (James 5:16). An early church manual from the year AD 100 instructs confession to happen *before* coming to the Lord's Table:

> On the Lord's own day, when you gather together, break bread and celebrate the eucharist *after you have confessed your unlawful deeds,* that your sacrifice may be pure . . . For this is the sacrifice mentioned by the Lord: "In every place and time, bring me a pure sacrifice. For I am a great King, says the Lord, and my name is considered marvelous among the Gentiles."[5]

> By confessing our sins, we wash our lives in the blood of the Lamb. Jesus Christ alone makes us worthy.

There it is. God is pure; He expects a pure sacrifice of praise. Yet who among us can offer that? No one. We come to His table with unclean hands. But by confessing our sins, we wash our lives in the blood of the Lamb. Jesus Christ alone makes us worthy.

Is it any surprise that liturgies of the Reformation era featured confession of sin in their worship services?[6]

Pastor-theologians like Martin Luther, John Calvin, and Thomas

Cranmer included the Ten Commandments near the beginning of their worship services, followed with an opportunity to confess the sins exposed by God's law. They knew that the grace of God for sinners is a central feature of authentic Christian worship.

Have you ever been cut to the heart by a convicting sermon? This can be a terrible experience at first. The Scripture being preached suddenly feels eerily relevant to something that happened in your life; the preacher makes an offhand comment that unknowingly exposes a secret you've been protecting; beads of sweat form on your brow; your pulse quickens—the Holy Spirit has pinned you to the wall. Ugh, this is no fun.

Yet if we don't run away from moments like this but stick with the process, marvelous things can happen. Our burdens can be removed, our lives can be transformed, and God can be glorified. For this reason a liturgical confession of sin is often placed after the sermon. Freshly convicted hearts can give way to kneeling contrition as congregations say together:

Most merciful God,
We confess that we have sinned against you
In thought, word, and deed,
By what we have done, and by what we have left undone.
We have not loved you with our whole heart;
We have not loved our neighbors as ourselves.
We are truly sorry and we humbly repent.
For the sake of your Son Jesus Christ,
Have mercy on us and forgive us;
That we may delight in your will, and walk in your ways,
To the glory of your name. Amen.[7]

A pastor can then impart the good news of the gospel:

Almighty God, our heavenly Father, who in his great mercy has promised forgiveness of sins to all those who sincerely repent and with true faith turn to him, have mercy upon you, pardon and deliver you from all your sins, confirm and strengthen you in all goodness, and bring you to everlasting life; through Jesus Christ our Lord. Amen.[8]

Sometimes this is followed by what some call "the Comfortable Words," meaning words of Scripture that bring comfort to stricken hearts. These include Jesus' invitation to the heavy-laden to receive His rest (Matt. 11:28), the trustworthy saying that Jesus Christ came into the world to save sinners (1 Tim. 1:15), and the famous lines from John 3:16.

After receiving God's forgiveness, we rise ready to come to Jesus' table with clean hands.

Often we need to verbally confess our sins to another Christian. No amount of liturgy can substitute for this vital person-to-person ministry. This is why many churches have prayer ministers, elders, pastors, and others who can privately pray with people before, during, and after a worship service.[9]

The Collects

Earlier this week my family had a bonfire with friends and family at Promontory Point, a public park overlooking Lake Michigan. Throughout the evening, my father-in-law would carefully place logs upon the fire to keep it burning at just the right temperature. These logs were solid, sure forms of fuel that served the whole group.

One feature of the ancient church is a short, compact form of prayer called a "collect" (from the Latin *collectio,* meaning "the act of collecting together"). We might think of collects as those expertly cut, carefully placed logs that keep us around the fire. They unify us in biblical prayers that burn at just the right temperature. While they are meant to be prayed by the pastor leading a worship service, that can be used in any setting of prayer or devotion.

Collects usually contain four elements: an invocation of God and His character; a petition that is grounded in God's character, a resulting consequence if that petition is granted, and giving God the glory or asking in His name.[10] Here is an example from one of my favorite collects:

> *Blessed Lord, who caused all holy Scriptures to be written for our learning: Grant us so to hear them, read, mark, learn, and inwardly digest them, that we may embrace and ever hold fast the blessed hope of everlasting life, which you have given us in our Savior Jesus Christ; who lives and reigns with you and the Holy Spirit, one God, for ever and ever. Amen.*[11]

The collect begins by invoking God's name and character: "Blessed Lord, who caused all holy Scriptures to be written for our learning." This is an affirmation of the apostle Paul's declaration in 2 Timothy 3:16 that all Scripture is God-breathed and profitable for instruction, reproof, correction, and equipping us for every good work. We are calling upon the same God who brought the Scriptures into existence.

Based on that truth, the collect makes a bold petition: "Grant us so to hear them, read, mark, learn, and inwardly digest them." It's

.... thing for God to ensure the writing of Scripture; it's another for us to actually read the Scriptures, internalizing them in our hearts and heads. We need God's help for that, too.

The third part of the collect describes what would result if our prayers were answered: "That we may embrace and ever hold fast the blessed hope of everlasting life, which you have given us in our Savior Jesus Christ." The result of learning the Scriptures is that we hold fast to the hope of glory. Suffering or temptation can loosen our grip and cause us to give up on the gospel. We need God's help to keep our noses in the Bible so we can keep our hope in Jesus.

How will all this happen? How will this prayer be answered? The fourth part of the collect clarifies this: through the mediation of our great High Priest, Jesus Christ, "who lives and reigns with you and the Holy Spirit, one God, for ever and ever. Amen." Each collect concludes in the name of Jesus, on whose merits we ask. Others also end by glorifying God in this final section.

If you are troubled by the work of evil in our day, feel the chill of the spiritual night we find ourselves in, and wonder if God will ever intervene to make things just and right again, I commend to you one of my favorite collects from the first Sunday of Advent:

> Almighty God, give us grace to cast away the works of darkness, and put on the armor of light, now in the time of this mortal life in which your Son Jesus Christ came to visit us in great humility; that in the last day, when he shall come again in his glorious majesty to judge both the living and the dead, we may rise to the life immortal; through him who lives and reigns with you and the Holy Spirit, one God, now and for ever. Amen.[12]

The Prayers of the People

Anxiety is fear on the inside that seeks control on the outside. For instance, our fear of disaster prompts us to make worst-case scenario plans. Or our fear of abandonment seeks to keep our loved ones in a close, enmeshed bond. In some cases, our fear of failure drives us to perfectionism in our work. In other cases, our fear of death keeps us "doomscrolling" through our news feed or social media for the next crisis. Anxiety runs through these situations like electricity. It keeps us overstimulated with the illusion that we are in control of the situations we fear the most. In the process, it gives us a racing heart, spinning mind, shallow breath, and other physical maladies.

> Anxiety is fear on the inside that seeks control on the outside.

Until we address it head-on, our anxiety will drive us into destructive behavior such as bingeing on substances, lashing out at scapegoats, burning out on work, or isolating ourselves in a state of catatonic shock. As we try to control the external world, our anxiety devours our interior soul. What's more, anxiety is contagious and can spread through families, congregations, and nations.[13] I don't have to tell you that this is happening on a massive, societal scale. How can we keep our heads as followers of Jesus?

I love the apostle Peter's gentle invitation: "Humble yourselves, therefore, under the mighty hand of God so that at the proper time he may exalt you, casting all your anxieties on him, because he cares for you" (1 Peter 5:6–7). If we are under the mighty hand of God, we may as well place all our anxiety into those massive and mighty hands. All things are under His control, not ours. What's more, He *cares*. He cares for *us*! He cares about the situations that terrify us, and God invites us to experience that care through our intercession.

The apostle Paul gives a similar exhortation: "I urge that supplications, prayers, intercessions, and thanksgivings for all people, for kings and all who are in high positions, that we may lead a peaceful and quiet life, godly and dignified in every way. . . . I desire then that in every place the men should pray, lifting holy hands without anger or quarreling" (1 Tim. 2:1–2, 8). Notice the emphasis here: as we lift up our voices and hands in prayer together, our lives can be marked by dignity, peace, and an absence of anger. We can't control how kings and people in high places act, yet we can pray for them. God is listening, and He can do things we cannot. Once we get this straight, anxiety tends to dwindle and the peace of God begins to rule in its place.

The earliest accounts of the church show us a praying church. "We all stand up together and send up prayers," recounted Justin Martyr in the second century; "the president likewise sends up prayers and thanksgivings to the best of his ability, and the people assent, saying the Amen."[14] Behind Justin's spare description is an intense, thriving life of intercession. Prayer was a matter of survival for people facing prison, sickness, demonic harassment, shipwrecks, robberies, discrimination, assault, and dire poverty.[15] One historian describes how much of a lifeline these prayers were for the Christians:

> The [early] Christians . . . found themselves involved in struggles with a systemic web of forces that they saw as evil—social,

spiritual, economic, religious, political. At times these forces persecuted them and attempted to humiliate, intimidate, and crush them. Nevertheless, during the early centuries the Christians gave the impression of being confidently powerful. Why? In part because they believed that the struggles they were involved in were above all spiritual.... The believers confessed ... that through the Holy Spirit, [God] had unleashed unimaginable spiritual power for good in the world. The Christians claimed that they had access to this power.[16]

Despite their lack of societal power, early Christians were confident in the power God delegated to them through united prayer. They took the words of Jesus seriously: "Where two or three are gathered in my name, there I am among them" (Matt. 18:20). Not only did it save them from disaster and harm, prayer propelled the believers back into danger with courage:

Prayer enabled them not only to cope with the dangers of day-to-day living but also to do joyfully the risky things that enabled the church to grow—to travel to new places, to touch plague victims, to see enemies as potential brothers. Christians' lives depended on their prayer, and they believed that the well-being of the empire, indeed of the world, did as well ... the prayer time was a power center of early Christian worship.[17]

Back to the present day: What makes you feel powerless? Are there thorny problems in your family, neighborhood, workplace, church, denomination, or school keeping you up at night? How about political trouble in your community or nation? Are you or someone you care about being harassed? Is money tight? Are medical problems (and the accompanying medical bills) piling up faster than you can keep up?

You and I are as vulnerable as those early Christians. We are also just as powerful when we assemble to pray in the name of Jesus. We too entrust the fate of empires and enemies, sickness and society, churches and culture, mothers and missionaries to the good care of a Sovereign Lord who is carefully listening to every single word we utter.

> We entrust the fate of empires and enemies, sickness and society, churches and culture, mothers and missionaries to the good care of a Sovereign Lord who is carefully listening to every single word we utter.

This is why many churches include "the Prayers of the People" in their worship services. This form of prayer covers many of the bases we might neglect: prayers for government, society, church leaders, the persecuted church, those in trouble or sickness, and the spread of the gospel. The leader of the prayers will pray for a particular issue, and then pause for others to pray silently (and in some cases, out loud).

Here's a sample:

Leader: *Almighty and ever-living God . . . we pray that you will lead the nations of the world in the way of righteousness; and so guide and direct their leaders, especially our President/Sovereign/Prime Minister, that your people may enjoy the blessings of freedom*

140

and peace. Grant that our leaders may impartially administer justice, uphold integrity and truth, restrain wickedness and vice, and protect true religion and virtue.[18]

That prayer might sound formal, and it is. Yet consider what might happen if God answered that prayer! Justice and integrity would flourish in public life. The nations of the world would go the way of righteousness. God would direct the leaders in key positions. This is a significant, biblical request we should pray with passion. What's more, there is also a space for people to add their own extemporaneous prayers based on the one prayed by the leader. Some may pray silently, others out loud in a whisper or a shout.

At some point, the leader prompts everyone to plead with God to hear the prayers they have prayed based on His mercy. The leader prays, "Lord, in Your mercy," and the people follow with, "Hear our prayer."

Imagine what might happen if we prayed about politics more than we posted about it on social media.

One of the most memorable Prayers of the People at Immanuel Anglican followed a tragic murder. Though our congregation was not directly involved, we walked into church deeply shaken by the violence and the events leading up to it. We were carrying deep sadness and anger in our hearts. You could feel the crackle and pop of anxiety in the room as we took our seats. When it came time for Prayers of the People, Christa (the prayer leader that day) prayed: "We pray for justice and for peace. Let mercy, love, and forgiveness enter where hatred, revenge, and fear are very real and present."

Christa then made space for people to respond. As is often the case with group prayer, it began with an awkward silence. Eventually someone chimed in with a prayer for justice. Soon after, someone cried out for God's presence and forgiveness. A deluge of passion followed. For about twenty-five minutes, the congregation lamented, pleaded with God, confessed sin, expressed their anger, and asked for renewal. It was one of the most raw, awkward, awe-filled times of prayer at our church. We left with a sense of Spirit-filled power to be Christ's ambassadors of peace. At the church picnic afterward, I remember the relief and joy on people's faces.

Maybe your church has a story like this, too. Some of my fellow Anglicans in Jos, Nigeria, are often praying in response to violence. Their daily prayer guide includes prayers for those whose businesses or homes have been bombed; for people without shelter, food, or safe drinking water; for those who have seen loved ones killed; and for orphans and widows and people who live in fear. When they gather in worship, leaders pray for God's mercy and justice to fall on corrupt politicians and terrorist organizations and corrupt military officials. Their passion is raw and unfiltered because war and injustice is their daily reality. Yet they leave worship ready to enter back into the danger in part because of this vital time of intercession.

Praying with Our Bodies

Ancient Christian prayer engages the body. This makes good biblical sense. Our Great High Priest is fully God, yes. Yet He is nothing less than a man who learned to pray with His body: crying loudly, shedding tears, and vocalizing His prayers and supplications (Heb. 4:14–5:10). Jesus passed through the heavens in a scarred, resurrected human body. When we approach His throne of grace, we bring our bodies, too.

Praying with our bodies makes good human sense, too. Behavior psychologists report that up to 93 percent of communication is nonverbal.[19] Like your mom always told you, it's not what you say, it's how you say it. Body language like eye rolling, gesturing wildly with your arms, hunching over, smiling, or shedding tears either underlines or undermines the words we speak.

In his spiritual allegory called *The Screwtape Letters*, C. S. Lewis imagines a high-ranking demon named Screwtape giving advice to Wormwood, a novice evil spirit. Screwtape is teaching Wormwood some well-established tips on keeping a Christian from spiritual maturity: "The best thing, where it is possible, is to keep the patient from the serious intention of praying altogether . . . At the very least, they can be persuaded that the bodily position makes no difference to their prayers; for they constantly forget, what you must always remember, that they are animals and that whatever their bodies do affects their souls."[20]

It's true. Even when we are not feeling particularly spiritual, we can lead with the body in prayer. Our soul tends to take the same position in which we place our bodies. This insight can help us offer ourselves to God more fully and resolutely.

There are four movements of prayer from the ancient church that any Christian can try. The first is *standing with raised arms*. An early church pastor named Origen encouraged Christians to pray standing, with arms raised in the air and eyes looking upward. This posture communicated that the believers were standing before the face of God, lifting up their needs to His care, as those who have been joined to Christ. The hands were reminiscent of Christ's cross, which they were ready to bear, and His innocence, which they had received by grace. [21]

Whether or not Christians raise their arms, standing up conveys a posture of spiritual readiness. Christians can stand during songs of praise, prayer, reciting the creed (itself a form of praise), and listening closely to the words of God. In many churches, worshipers stand for the reading of the gospel. Standing teaches us to be alert and attentive to the activity of God.

> Standing teaches us to be alert and attentive to the activity of God.

Kneeling is especially appropriate for the confession of sin. Kneeling is a humble posture that communicates our need for mercy. Biblical examples include people kneeling before Jesus as they make a request (Matt. 17:14; 20:20; Mark 1:40) or kneeling in prayer (Acts 21:5).

Bowing is closely related to kneeling, as it communicates deference, humility, and respect before a greater authority. Bowing can be a slight bend at the neck, or a deeper bow from the waist. A mainstay in Eastern culture, bowing is largely an unfamiliar practice in the West. Scripture calls us to bow down before the Lord our maker (Ps. 95:6) and warns us against bowing down to false gods (Ex. 20:4–5) or even angels (Rev. 19:10).

Bowing in Christian worship is a way to recognize the authority of Jesus Christ, displayed on the cross and vindicated by the resurrection. Thus, many Christians bow to a physical cross that is processed or displayed in a worship service. They are not worshiping that cross as an idol; they are worshiping Jesus. The physical cross serves as an important visual cue that Christ's unseen presence is near. One may also bow at the mention of the name of Jesus during worship. We will all bow at the name of Jesus and confess Him as Lord over heaven and earth at the end of history (Phil. 2:9-11). We who confess Him as King may as well begin bowing now.

Making the sign of the cross is the prayer action that might feel the most controversial to some, since it is closely associated with Roman Catholicism and Eastern Orthodoxy. Some construe the sign of the cross as a superstitious act of dead religion. You might be surprised to know that the sign of the cross began in the early church as a way to secretly identify yourself as a Christian in times of persecution.[22] By drawing a tiny invisible cross shape on your forehead with your thumb, you could say to other Christians, "I belong to Jesus Christ." Uninitiated outsiders would not think twice since this could also be seen as scratching or rubbing your forehead. Christians would use the sign of the cross in dangerous situations where they could not pray out loud but still needed God's help and protection. No matter what trial or

> Bowing in Christian worship is a way to recognize the authority of Jesus Christ, displayed on the cross and vindicated by the resurrection.

temptation awaited them, they could cry out to God with a small physical action that symbolized the silent prayer from their heart.

This small gesture also became a Christian way of life. Around AD 200, a pastor named Tertullian described how his flock wove this prayer into the fabric of their physical lives: "At every forward step and movement, at every going in and out, when we put on our clothes and shoes, when we bathe, when we sit at table, when we light the lamps, on couch, on seat, in all the ordinary actions of daily life, we trace upon the forehead the sign."[23]

Though our lives might be different from our spiritual forebears, we still bathe, put on shoes and clothes, and sit at tables and couches. We also face trials and temptations, headaches and heartbreaks, and housework. All the while we share a calling to glorify God in the bodies that God has given us and that Jesus has redeemed. Why not take up this prayer action to set apart every aspect of our life in the body to the Lord?

As you can imagine, the sign of the cross was also used in worship gatherings. As the centuries progressed and the numbers of the faithful swelled, church leaders ran into a new problem: people could not see them making the sign of the cross from the back rows. So the pastors leading services expanded the sign of the cross. Instead of simply smudging out a tiny cross on their foreheads, they would draw a larger cross in the air, high enough for all to see. Christians began to trace a cross upon their bodies, using their right hand from forehead to chest, and then from shoulder to shoulder.[24]

When making the sign of the cross, we identify ourselves with two profound Christian realities: the cross of Christ and the

Trinity. When we hear the words "in the name of the Father, Son and Holy Spirit" we can affirm our belief in the Trinity by making the sign of the cross. Or when we hear the words "Jesus is Lord," we can pay homage to Him through the same action. As we do, the prayer in our heart can simply be, "Lord, I belong to You; set me apart."

Incense

We hear the gospel with our ears in the sermon, taste it with our mouths in the Eucharistic meal, touch it with our hands in the passing of the peace, and see it with our eyes when someone is baptized. That's four senses down, one to go. What about *smelling* the gospel?

Some churches choose to burn incense in their worship services. The incense is lit in a small ornate container known as a censer (sometimes called a "thurible"), which hangs by a series of chains so the entire apparatus can be carried and swung throughout the church. As incense is added to a charcoal base, the smoke and smell arises and can fill an entire room. Before the era of modern hygiene and sanitation, incense served the practical purpose of covering up any unsavory smells that could distract from worship.[25] Yet in the Old and New Testaments, incense also served as a powerful symbol of the presence of God among His people (1 Kings 8:10–11; Isa. 6:6–8) as well as the prayers of the faithful ascending up to God's throne room (Ps. 141:2; Rev. 5:8; 8:3–4).[26]

Given that incense can be both seen and smelled, it serves as a powerful and sometimes polarizing element in worship. Smells can create and recall memories (whether old perfumes or Mom's home cooking). So for those with a memory of pagan worship, as in the case of the early church, incense was more of a distraction than an aid to worship. Later in the fourth century, Christians began to use it more regularly.[27] One helpful way to think about incense is like a family custom. Some choose to use it and find it to help their worship of Jesus. Others use it only on special occasions, like Christmas or Easter, and many choose not to use incense at all. The bottom line is that our common prayer to God is like incense; when we pray in Jesus' name, He finds our prayers to be a sweet-smelling aroma. Just as we are provoked by a powerful smell, God is provoked by our prayers (Rev. 8:1–5).

The Unfailing Power of Prayer

On May 19, 1897, the great Bible expositor Charles Spurgeon preached a sermon from Revelation 8 to wake his London congregation from their spiritual torpor. As in our time, the people of his church experienced their fair share of troubles and threats. As in our lives, they probably struggled to keep praying in faith amidst injustice, sickness, and the invisible, slow nature of God's kingdom. Yet when they came together, Spurgeon considered their intercession to be of greater worth than his highly prized sermons. I cannot think of a better way to conclude this chapter than the rousing words of this barrel-chested British preacher. And as you read them, remember that holy bonfire.

> And now, lastly, brethren, let us blend our prayers, however faulty and feeble they may be, with the general supplications of

the period . . . O church of God, cry day and night unto him . . . let not thy voice be silent; but cry, and even in the night watches pour out thy heart like water before the Lord thy God. And, dearly beloved, remember that prayer is effectual with God.

When the censer of God's church shall have been well filled with prayer . . . then will come voices declaring Christ. Then will come thunderings, for with the Gospel will go the voice of God, which is like thunder, louder than the voice of man. Then will flash forth lightnings, for the light of God's power and truth will come forth with majesty, and men's hearts shall be smitten with it, and made obedient to it. And then shall earthquakes shake society, till the thrones of despots reel . . . till the land that could not be ploughed with the gospel plough shall be broken up with secret heavings from the eternal God.

We have but to pray. All things are possible to us. Pray, brethren. You have the key in the door of heaven, keep it there and turn it till the gate shall open. Pray, brethren, for prayer holds the chain which binds the old dragon. Prayer can hold fast and restrain even Satan himself. Pray. God girds you with omnipotence, if you know how to pray. May we not fail here, but may the Spirit of God strengthen us, and to God shall be glory for ever and ever. Amen.[28]

IX

MISSION

FOR THE LIFE OF THE WORLD

Right before the end of the service, many liturgical churches end
with a "post-Communion prayer." Here's the Anglican version:

> Heavenly Father,
> We thank you for feeding us with the spiritual food
> Of the most precious Body and Blood
> Of your Son our Savior Jesus Christ;
> And for assuring us in these holy mysteries
> That we are living members of the body of your Son,
> And heirs of your eternal Kingdom.
> And now, Father, send us out to do the work you have given us
>   to do,
> To love and serve you as faithful witnesses of Christ our Lord.

To him, to you, and to the Holy Spirit,
Be honor and glory, now and forever, Amen.[1]

This prayer captures well how worship flows into mission. As we are united with God through Christ, we are sent by God as His faithful witnesses of Christ our Lord. We are family members, once estranged and hostile, now reconnected at the table. We are at the end of the meal, well-fed and deeply encouraged. Our hearts are full, our doubts assuaged. Now we are ready to push our seats back, stand up, and set our own table for those who have no place to belong. We are hopeful that like us, they too can become living members of the body of Jesus Christ. In the words of Lesslie Newbigin, our "mission begins with an explosion of joy."[2]

So we pray, "Now, Father, *send us out*." Send us like You sent Abraham to a land he did not know (Gen. 12). Like him, we want to inherit the nations for Your glory. Send us out like You sent the Twelve to proclaim the kingdom, push back evil and heal the broken (Luke 9). Send us out like You sent the seventy-two— without knapsacks or purses, to see Satan fall like lightning (Luke 10). Send us out like You sent the eleven to the ends of the earth (Matt. 28:16–20). We know You will be with us, to the very end of the age.

In some churches, this post-Communion prayer is followed by a "recessional"—one final worship song that allows the cross to be carried from the front of the sanctuary to the exit, followed by the clergy and leaders. The symbolism of the recessional is that *Jesus is leading us out* of these four walls—not to the coffee (okay, maybe for a few minutes) but to our calling. Jesus is leading us out where the harvest is plentiful and so are the dangers.

We follow the cross into uncertainty and exposure, miracles and perils, enemies and people of peace. It's only natural that we would linger at the coffee for a while. Sometimes we are tempted to participate in the liturgical action of following the cross without following through with the missional living it implies.

This was certainly true for me. In the twelve years since my first ministry burnout experience, the Lord had restored my soul, healed my heart, provided key mentors, even provided a church-planting residency that helped me develop ministry skills in a supportive yet dynamic environment. As the residency was wrapping up, I was hoping to take a position at a wonderful church on the East Coast. Not only would I get to learn under another great leader, I could also move my family out of the urban center for more space and kid-friendly amenities.

Yet another invitation—one less secure and a heck of a lot more scary—would not let me rest: "Come back to Chicago to plant an Anglican church." I had no interest in this; there was too much risk and responsibility and too little assurance of it working out. Yet while visiting the East Coast church, the Holy Spirit would not leave me alone. Sitting in the service, I had a sense of disquiet and desolation. I wanted to work at this church, and I wanted to move to this community. Yet I sensed the Lord was saying no.

Flipping around in my Bible, I landed in Acts 9, the famous "Road to Damascus" story of Saul encountering the risen Lord. I was arrested by these words: "I am Jesus, whom you are persecuting. But rise and enter the city, and you will be told what you are to do" (Acts 9:5–6). The authority of Jesus, originally blinding

Saul, captured me also in a fresh way. "I am Jesus"—the Lord, glorious and full of authority, yet also so kind and near that He would identify Himself completely with His suffering church. This same Jesus was asking me to go into the city, not to leave it, and imparting a promise to lead every step of the way.

> My first obstacle to following Jesus into His mission was my own heart.

My first obstacle to following Jesus into His mission was my own heart: too much fear and self-regard, too little love and courage. I did not need any more sermons about mission, songs about mission, or even more liturgy about mission. I needed to *go* on the mission: say yes to church planting, look for a Chicago apartment for a family of five (soon to be six. We got turned down by many landlords!), meet with leaders on the ground, and pray, pray, pray—and fast. This was all possible once I let go of my cherished dreams of comfort and my need to control outcomes.

One of the pitfalls of embracing the historic, ancient forms of church is that the roots of worship go deep, but the fruit of mission never seems to appear. We can become so enamored with liturgy, sacraments, theology, art, creeds, and even prayer that we have no energy left for the very thing it equips us for: being faithful witnesses of Jesus Christ. Worse, we can even grow smug in a boutique, sophisticated Christianity and look down on efforts to engage and reach people who are uninitiated. May the Lord protect us from becoming protective and insular and from hearts that grow cold and self-preserving.

The ancient gifts of the church are not collector's items. They are mission-critical supplies for a life-and-death rescue operation. They are powerful, tangible signs of God's kingdom, which is moving aggressively to throw off Satan's cruel regime of hell and death and enslavement.

J. R. R. Tolkien helps us understand this better in his story *The Fellowship of the Ring*. In their quest to destroy the Ring of Power, Frodo and his companions encounter Galadriel, a powerful elf who lives in Lothlorien. After a period of refreshment and reflection, they are ready to depart, and Galadriel equips them with gifts tailored to their quest. She supplies the whole company with *lembas*, an elvish bread that would strengthen their bodies and souls as they marched to Mordor. She further outfits them with enchanted cloaks to shield them from enemies.

> The ancient gifts of the church are mission-critical supplies for a life-and-death rescue operation.

To Sam, she supplies an elvish rope, which yields completely to Sam's wishes on the dangerous climbs ahead. To Frodo, Galadriel supplied her most powerful gift: the Phial of Galadriel, with the benediction: "May it be a light to you in dark places, when all other lights go out."[3] Frodo and Sam will weaponize the Phial against the demonic monster known as Shelob, who attempts to block their passage and swallow them in her foul web of spiritual darkness. As Frodo and Sam lift up the Phial with courage, its light pushes Shelob back, wounding her with heavenly terror.[4]

el's gifts play a critical role in their confrontation with evil, saving Middle Earth.

The Lord Jesus has equipped His church with everything she needs to fulfill her mission. Our most precious gift is the gospel: the promise of union with Him through His death and resurrection, the forgiveness of sins, the gift of His Spirit (John 14:15–31) and the promise of His enduring presence until the mission is complete (Matt. 28:16–20). What's more, He's given His church gifted leaders and ministers (Eph. 4:11–12), a seat at His Communion table (Luke 22:14–23), and a share in His baptism (Rom. 6).

> The Lord Jesus has equipped His church with everything she needs to fulfill her mission. Our most precious gift is the gospel.

None of these gifts may be hoarded, lest we forget how precious they are. The inheritance of the gospel, as well as the tangible gifts of the church, are for us to display, share, and wield. Take the Eucharist, for instance. The mission of God is baked, as it were, into the Communion bread. Christ is revealed to us when we partake of it in faith. As we are welcomed at His table by grace, we can likewise open our table to those outside the church. In the words of one observer of the ancient church: "They have a common table, but not a common bed."[5] It turns out that hospitality to outsiders, both inside and outside of Sundays, is one of the most effective forms of evangelism in our day, too. In his book *You Found Me: New Research on How Unchurched Nones, Millennials, and Irreligious Are Surprisingly Open to Christian Faith*, Rick Richardson found that hospitality is "the most important predictive factor of churches becoming conversion communities" (meaning, churches where non-Christians regularly come to faith).[6]

Everything beautiful and good inside the church become weapons of warfare outside the church, pushing back the darkness, blessing people far from God. This includes gospel proclamation, healing ministries, small groups, liturgy, art, help for marriages and families, and discipleship. Whatever good things we have received from the Lord, we pass on. The church is best when she is on offense.

Our family moved back to Chicago to plant an Anglican church. As the "launch team" of our church coalesced in that first year, we were practicing mission and preparing to launch weekly services in the Uptown neighborhood. But we faced a big problem: we needed a worship space. We were about to outgrow the current meeting hall we had been using, and we had less than two months to find an alternative. Door after door was closed to us. So we entered into a forty-day period of fasting and praying. We focused our prayers for the Lord to move through our community to bless our city and for a worship space.

Exactly one week into that forty-day period, tragedy struck: five people in the neighborhood were critically wounded in a hail of bullets from an automatic weapon. This happened outside a church-run food pantry just a half block from where our church plant was meeting on Sundays to pray and plan. The shock of the news hit us hard: this is not a game! And this was one of the moments when Jesus came through on His promise that "you will be told what you are to do." The morning after the shooting we scrapped our plans for a staff meeting and quickly organized a noonday prayer gathering across the street from the scene of the shooting.

We put the word out and showed up with our Bibles, prayer books, and song sheets. Members of the community, including one of the shooting victims, saw us assembling and decided to join us. I remember how that victim of the shooting's voice shook with emotion as he read this collect from the prayer book: "Lord Jesus Christ, you said to your apostles, 'Peace I give to you; my peace I leave with you:' Regard not our sins, but the faith of your Church, and give to us the peace and unity of that heavenly city, where with the Father and the Holy Spirit you live and reign, now and forever. Amen."[7]

Our worship leader, Dan Fager, brought his guitar and played his achingly beautiful song, "Branch of the Lord," originally written for the Easter Vigil. The lyrics are from Isaiah 4:2–6:

On that day, the Branch of the Lord will be beautiful and glorious.
The fruit of the land will be the pride and glory of Israel's survivors . . .
There will be a canopy over all the glory
And there will be a booth for shade from the heat by day
And a refuge and shelter from storm and rain.[8]

Someone else read the Scripture for the day, and I preached the gospel as best I knew how, what with the street noise, the caution tape, and especially the specter of violence and the sadness and pain in all our hearts. This noonday prayer was our way of saying: "No, hell, you cannot have the final word over this corner of Chicago. Jesus is Lord, and He will make it right. Here is a foretaste." The whole experience was uncomfortable, yet we had a sense that this is exactly where God had sent us: out in the community, in painfully broken situations, armed with the healing gifts of the church.

A ready-made church building may well have robbed us of this opportunity, and with it the attunement to the needs of the people around us. By the time launch Sunday rolled around, and we had a building to meet in, we folded this and other experiences into our ministry. "I felt very exposed on that corner," Dan (the worship leader) later reflected. "I was used to 'ministry' within the safe confines of a building. But it was a disorienting experience in a good way."[9] Whether sharing the gospel with a neighbor, adopting an orphan, planting a new church, or starting a medical clinic in an underserved neighborhood, mission often feels vulnerable. Our contributions can seem so small in comparison with the need. Yet like the promise in Psalm 126, when we go out weeping with the humble seeds of the gospel and gifts of the church, we can expect that we will return, eventually, bringing in the sheaves of the harvest with

> The church is at her best when she is on offense, courageously pushing back darkness, humbly shining the light of Christ, planting seeds of the gospel wherever there are ears to hear.

shouts of joy. Our weakness is powerful in the hands of God.

The church is at her best not when she is playing defense, protective and cloistered. She is best when she is on offense, courageously pushing back darkness, humbly shining the light of Christ, planting seeds of the gospel wherever there are ears to hear. The church needs the mission of God. We need the Lord to answer that post-Communion prayer, "Now, Father, send us out" with a gentle, firm shove: "Your prayers have been answered, now out you go!"

God's Mission Features the Church

The church needs God's mission to stay healthy and vital. What then? Should the mission leave the church behind? After all, the local church has a credibility problem: too often she has failed to live up to her own standards, preaching Jesus while living like the rest of the world. Too many church leaders have fallen; too many elder boards have misbehaved or abnegated; too many congregations have been stiff-necked. What's more, churches can be out of step, answering questions no one is asking anymore or running ministries that have run out of steam. One time I asked a young woman in Chicago if she would ever consider darkening the doors of a church. "No way," she said, "churches seem to live in an alternative universe, with no connection to my life and world at all."

Could we responsibly bring people exploring Christianity to the local church? Could the mission just do without her? Maybe we could lead people to Jesus, even His kingdom in a broad sense, but not to the scandal-filled local body of believers. Otherwise, she might just block the winds of the Spirit.

Deconstruction has become the work-around for many people to solve this problem. They love Jesus but have so much church-related pain and suspicion that their lives and mission become un-tethered from her altogether. The deconstruction process involves questioning what church leaders have taught us, and discarding old beliefs, structures, and people that used to form the fabric of our faith. Eventually, we move on to something more authentic, healthy, and pure—at least in theory.

You might be surprised to know that Jesus Himself led His disciples through a process of deconstruction. They came into His circle with all kinds of stubborn expectations for Him, His king-dom, and the outcomes of their mission. Mostly they hoped for a non-crucified king of Israel, when in fact Jesus was destined to be a quite-crucified King for people from every tribe, tongue, people, and nation. Like us, the disciples wanted power and control, not persecution and crosses. Jesus deconstructed this with patient correction and finally with His own cross. Whether cleansing the temple (Mark 11:15–19) or correcting false assumptions (Luke 24:13–49), it's fair to say that Jesus stands ready to deconstruct idols, unjust structures, non-biblical expectations, and anything unholy or untrue. It's a healthy, normal part of our faith maturation.

Yet the one reality that Jesus does not deconstruct? His bride, the church. Sure, He may reform her (Rev. 2–3) and purify her (Eph. 5:25–27). Yet He does not abandon, divorce, or dismantle her. In fact, Jesus *builds* and *fills* and *empowers* His church for her mission. "I will build my church, and the gates of hell shall not prevail against it" (Matt. 16:18). Even more, Paul tells us that the Father gave His Son to the church, "which is his body, the fullness of him who fills all in all" (Eph. 1:23). That's right: just as the fullness of God is pleased to dwell in Jesus (Col. 2:9), the fullness of Jesus is pleased to dwell in His church.[10] This is why Jesus became the spotless Lamb who was slain: to win for Himself a spotless Bride, bone of His bone, flesh of His flesh. As my friend Scott says, if you want to see Jesus in this life, you cannot look over the shoulder of His local church.

Each convert in the book of Acts was instructed to make connection to the local assembly of believers for baptism and discipleship. We see this foretold in the Great Commission: "Go therefore and make disciples of all nations, baptizing them in the name of the Father and of the Son and of the Holy Spirit, teaching them to observe all that I have commanded you. And behold, I am with you always, to the end of the age" (Matt. 28:18–20). There's a virtuous cycle here: Jesus sends us, His church, out on mission. The result is that people come to faith. When that happens, the mission becomes a new church, or flows back into an existing one. The process repeats, and the presence of Jesus is at the center, holding all of it together. You can find Him in the confines of a touchable, sendable, joinable, sacramental community of believers.

There is a time to tear down, and a time to build up (Eccl. 3:3). At some point, Jesus' disciples transitioned from deconstruction to devotion. That devotion included the wholehearted participation in the apostles' teaching, the Communion meal, the prayers, and the koinonia (sharing of homes, meals, and possessions). They expected to meet God in the Scriptures, sacraments, prayers, and sacrificial life (Acts 2:42–47). Building up the local church is not always constructing an idol; sometimes it is building an altar to the living God. As we have seen in the stories and history of the early church, this was a worthy place for new converts to find their way to God, and salvation.

Have you ever met someone enamored by an ideal spouse or romantic partner? They can piece together a perfect archetype: virtuous, beautiful, enchanting, possessed of every rare and attractive feature without any flaws. This phantom then becomes the impossible ideal no human can attain. Idealized romance often cuts short actual romantic opportunities.

The same can be true of churches. Missiologist Stefan Paas notes that "Christian identity (outside the church) often assumes a gnostic character: the individual bonds with an invisible, spiritual church or with an idealistic kingdom of God, without engaging with a concrete, human community of Christ in a local congregation that is connected with other congregations."[11] These church ideals can give us license to run and hide, ghosting the church as we would a romantic interest after an awkward date.

A better way might be the ancient path: devotion on the other end of deconstruction. What if we spent our energies building up the church using the gifts God gave us, humbly serving her, joining her mission, confident that Jesus can meet us?

If we are to devote ourselves to Jesus' church or His mission, many of us will have to account for our cynicism. Deacon Susan Raedeke likens cynicism to the "Snuggie" blanket, which was made famous in TV ads.[12] Snuggies are wearable blankets that make you want to sit on the couch, giving the wearer a comfortable distance from any devoted activity happening in the house.

> What if we spent our energies building up the church using the gifts God gave us, humbly serving her, joining her mission, confident that Jesus can meet us?

Cynicism can be like that. It keeps us comfortable, safely distant, and inactive. After we have been hurt, especially by someone with more power than us, cynicism is a temptation. Author Paul Miller says that "Cynicism begins with the wry assurance that everyone has an angle. . . . The cynic is always observing, critiquing but never engaged, loving, and hoping. To be cynical is to be distant . . . it leads to a creeping bitterness that can deaden . . . and even destroy the spirit."[13]

Yes, some church cultures are toxic. Some church leaders are abusive. Some church people are nasty. Some church boards are controlling. Yet, thanks be to God, that is not always the case. Some church cultures are healthy, some church leaders are humble, some church people are kind and generous, and some church boards are wise and trusting. How do we distinguish, how do we know whom to trust, especially after getting hurt?

Holy discernment can help us. Jesus even told us to practice this when He said, "Beware of false prophets, who come to you in sheep's clothing but inwardly are ravenous wolves" (Matt. 7:15–20). Wolves exist. Bullying sheep exist. You will know them by their track record. This is holy discernment; it takes skill and grace.

Cynicism is more of a blunt instrument, holding all human beings to be suspect. Cynicism can lead us to believe that God simply cannot work through human beings—only through trees, rivers, silence, and our own inner voice. We assume the Holy Spirit cannot speak through women or men, and certainly not through leaders, ministers, pastors, or others with influence.

Yet in the ancient church we find there to be awe and wonder, rather than cynicism, in response to the apostles. "Awe came upon every soul, and many wonders and signs were being done through the apostles" (Acts 2:43). The awe is not at the apostles but at the Lord Jesus who is working through them by grace. Jesus does not cast away human beings, but redeems them, purifies them, and empowers them. He wants us to receive and give ministry to each other and from each other. According to the prophet Joel, the day of the Lord is marked by people who prophesy and dream—both young and old (Joel 2:28).

> If the church is to stand in our day, we need grace to trust each other, work together, and lift each other up.

If the church is to stand in our day, we need grace to trust each other, work together, and lift each other up. The church is not meant to be leaderless and gift-less, everyone wrapped in a Snuggie rehashing the bad old days. The future of the church is not on the couch but on our knees, in awe and wonder as God works new creation through His women and men.

"And the Lord added to their number day by day those who were being saved" (Acts 2:47). Isn't that a beautiful picture of

...he mission of God flowing back into the church? It's His mission, His church, His people. Remember the prayer following Communion?

> *Heavenly Father,*
> *We thank you for feeding us with the spiritual food*
> *Of the most precious Body and Blood*
> *Of your Son our Savior Jesus Christ;*
> *And for assuring us in these holy mysteries*
> *That we are living members of the body of your Son,*
> *And heirs of your eternal Kingdom.*
> *And now, Father, send us out to do the work you have given us to do,*
> *To love and serve you as faithful witnesses of Christ our Lord.*
> *To him, to you, and to the Holy Spirit,*
> *Be honor and glory, now and forever, Amen.*[14]

We are *living members* of the body of Jesus Christ. Like the believers in Acts, we are sent; we multiply; we go in Jesus' name to heal, to be faithful witnesses of the gospel. Earth is filled with heaven, first in Jesus, now in His Body. So we "go forth into the world in peace, rejoicing in the power of the Spirit."[15] As the Father sent the Son, so now the Son sends us: for the life of the world and the glory of God.

Out we go.

X

COURAGE

FAITHFULNESS IN CRISIS

Shortly after her twenty-first birthday, Princess Elizabeth Windsor—known later as Queen Elizabeth II—addressed a group of young Christians with this stirring challenge:

> When you and I were confirmed we were commissioned to be witnesses to the truth of the Gospel of Our Lord Jesus Christ. A witness is one who speaks of that which he knows about first hand. We need to have such a knowledge of our faith that we can be bold in our witness and adventurous in our living. . . . We know that we shall probably be in a minority wherever we are. We know we shall have to face insecurity, opposition, and perhaps danger, for the confession of our faith. But the Christian Church has always prospered in adversity, and we must certainly not be afraid.[1]

By calling us to a life of courage, Her Majesty's words echo that of Jesus, His apostles, and the example of the early church. As C. S. Lewis once noted, courage is not merely one of the virtues, but each of the virtues at their testing point.[2] It's one thing to appreciate the creeds and ceremonies from our spiritual forebearers; it's quite another to emulate their courage under fire. Even if a "high church" approach to Christianity is not your cup of tea, please consider with me the pattern of faithfulness set by our cloud of witnesses. Because when our allegiance to Jesus Christ puts us at odds with the powers of this age, our faith will be tested. After a season of relative ease, that testing can seem like a rude interruption to our sugar plum dreams of peace and prosperity.

This may have well been the case for Cyprian, a thirty-something African pastor less than a year into a new ministry assignment. Cyprian was an adult convert to Christianity. His career as a talented public speaker and teacher had earned him a gilded life of fame and fortune. Unable to satisfy his hunger for meaning through sex and wine, Cyprian was drawn to the enduring joy of the Christians in his hometown of Carthage. A faithful pastor named Caecilianus shared the gospel with Cyprian, who upon conversion sold his property and distributed the money to the poor. A year later Cyprian entered pastoral ministry. When his predecessor suddenly died, Cyprian was made a bishop over Carthage in AD 249.

Soon after his election to this role, several crises landed in Cyprian's lap. The first was religious persecution: by decree of the new Roman Emperor Decius, all Christians were required to pay formal, public homage to the gods. Non-compliance meant imprisonment, torture, loss of property, or even death. Many Christians, especially Christian leaders, lost their lives through cruel and unusual punishment. Others capitulated under pressure, many immediately regretting their decision. This led to a second crisis: conflict and polarization within the church. "Lapsed" or "fallen" Christians begged for reentry to the community, while the "confessors" who had paid dearly for their faithfulness wanted to keep them out for their betrayal. If this was not enough, a third crisis threatened to extinguish the Carthaginian church altogether: a deadly, violent plague that ravaged the population.[3]

Going Back to Go Forward

Persecution. Polarization. Pandemic. How could Cyprian possibly be faithful in such an environment? How could any of us? Yet it was crises like these that birthed some of the best moments for the church. This was not because of superior technique or brilliant strategizing, but because the power of the gospel flowed through the church's flawed, faithful people of God.

I will offer three postures from the ancient church that we can adopt in any generation and apply to any crisis—not to further burden already weary Christians but to encourage and inspire.

> The power of the gospel flowed through the church's flawed, faithful people of God.

Willing to Die

The first posture of ancient Christians is that *they were willing to suffer and die publicly*. Many demonstrated a courage as contagious as the plagues they faced. Ignatius of Antioch (not to be confused with the Ignatius from Loyola) was appointed as a church leader around AD 100, taking the baton soon after the apostles. First and foremost, Ignatius wanted to be Christ's true disciple. His pastoral leadership flowed out of that commitment. So when he was sentenced to death by Roman authorities, he understood his martyrdom to be the capstone project of his apprenticeship to Jesus.

As ten Roman soldiers escorted Ignatius from Syria to his execution in Rome, he wrote gripping pastoral letters to the churches he would greet along the way. In one letter, Ignatius begs the Christians in Rome to not intervene in his case: "I am willingly dying for God, unless you hinder me. I urge you . . . allow me to be bread for the wild beasts; through them I am able to attain to God. I am the wheat of God and am ground by the teeth of the wild beasts, that I may be found to be the pure bread of Christ . . . Then I will truly be a disciple of Jesus Christ."[4]

His confidence in the coming judgment, as well as the glorious resurrection for those in Christ, was on display in his letter to the Ephesian church: "In him [Jesus] I am bearing my chains, which are spiritual pearls; in them I hope to rise again, through your prayer."[5]

Notice how Ignatius described his impending death. His chains? Pearls. The teeth of the wild beasts? A grinding mill, making him like fresh bread for God. This would be too macabre were it not for his fearless, resolute trust in the resurrection.

Jesus had defeated death in His cross and resurrection. For early Christians, death was but a gateway into life. They didn't have to fear plague, disaster, martyrdom, or the beasts. In fact, the greater danger was loving this world too much.

Ignatius's secret weapon in crisis was his surrender to Christ's will for his life and ministry. He held nothing back; his very body was on the altar of worship to God. Because of this, his pastoral ministry carried great authority, even after his death. Ignatius's final journey to martyrdom was a passion play, a gospel sermon being preached and demonstrated in real time. His letters were the sermon, and his life was the visual aid.

Crises have their way of revealing the true motives of a follower of Jesus. Jesus Himself taught about this using the metaphor about a shepherd, sheep, and an approaching wolf. He describes how the arrival of the wolf—an existential crisis for a flock of sheep—tends to clarify who is a true shepherd and who is a hired hand: "The good shepherd lays down his life for the sheep. He who is a hired hand and not a shepherd, who does not own the sheep, sees the wolf coming and leaves the sheep and flees, and the wolf snatches them and scatters them. He flees because he is a hired hand and *cares nothing for the sheep*" (John 10:11–13).

Hired hands care nothing for the sheep of God entrusted to them. They treat the sheep as nuisances to be avoided or resources to be fleeced. In the end, they just don't care. When a crisis comes, a hired hand usually runs for cover instead of staying to suffer.

Tim Laniak is a Bible scholar who spent significant time living and working with shepherds in Jordan, Israel, and the Sinai. He tells the story of the Aref family who live in the Jordanian mountains and care for a flock of sheep. One night, a frightening storm blew through and the tents collapsed around the animals. The animals immediately bolted into the darkness. A good shepherd would have run after them. Unfortunately, the shepherd they hired for the night watch cared more for his own survival than the flock—so he ran for cover.

The entire Aref family went out in the darkness and thunderstorm, keeping their balance on the slick rocks. As they climbed, they called out for their sheep. They didn't sleep until they found every last one and got them under protection and shelter.

The next day they tracked down the hired hand, who was hiding in the next village behind an oven, and promptly fired him. Why? The crisis proved he was not a true shepherd.[6]

Our willingness to suffer—even die—for our Christian faith answers a fundamental question: *Why are we Christ followers in the first place?* Are we truly walking with Christ out of love for Him and His church? Or are we in it for less noble reasons: social connections, image management, peer pressure (including family pressure), comfort, or a way to have a more successful life? Truth be told, most of us are a blend of contradictions, including good and not-so-good motives. Like Ignatius, we are learning to be Christ's true disciples. A healthy Christian can admit that, receive grace and allow the testing of their faith to purify their inner motivations.

> Our willingness to suffer for our Christian faith answers a fundamental question: *Why are we Christ followers in the first place?*

Ignatius's example included a dramatic martyrdom—that was his calling, and he fulfilled it. Most of us have a less clear and dramatic path in giving our lives away. Every Christian will have a fair share of "miniature" death-and-resurrection experiences. This was certainly the case for Cyprian, the orator-turned-bishop. After the Emperor's decree that Christians pay homage to the gods, Cyprian went into hiding. He discerned that his time had not yet come, as his flock needed his leadership to endure the crisis. So he pastored through letters, which have survived to this day. As a result of his exile, the pastors serving under him used the opportunity to savage his reputation: "How can you trust him? He ran away!" Many of them were still seething from his election to bishop. Even as he navigated his first crisis, Cyprian had to endure leadership sabotage from within his own ranks.[7]

This is the more common way to embrace suffering in the Christian life: making a difficult decision that many will not understand, taking heat for that decision, and doing so for the sake of Jesus and His people. Every follower of Jesus with a beating heart will eventually suffer a broken heart. They will pour their lives out like a drink offering. Anglicans call this an "oblation"; Jesus calls it love. When we face crises with a willingness to love God with all our heart, soul, and mind and love our neighbor as ourselves, everything goes on the altar: energy, reputations, money, outcomes, personal space, belongings, personal time, preferences, and all those sugar-plum dreams.

This is not to say Christians become doormats or non-persons. Heroes like Ignatius and Cyprian show us that the opposite is true: sacrificial love makes our lives more distinct and interesting.

ⴑⴄristians with clear values and gospel mettle have the personal strength to choose suffering, including death and everything that leads up to it. We can be as confident as Ignatius that a resurrection will follow every death or "mini-death": a stronger soul, a greater capacity for love and joy, spiritual endurance, and a more resilient, unshakable trust in the Lord. We can get free from needing all that surface-level love or affirmation from the people in our lives. Paradoxically, this leaves us more capable of loving them as a result.

So, reader, you have a crisis on your hands. You didn't ask for this. You feel the panic growing, and you're looking for answers. Take a deep breath; the Lord is with you. He will never forsake you. He's in this with you, to the end of the age, even if it means your death. If you trust Him, no irredeemable harm will befall you—that's a promise from the Good Shepherd Himself (Rom. 8:28). Confess the part of you that wants to preserve life, money, relationships, reputation, control, whatever. Ask Him where your sacrifice is best put to use. Tell Him how much you love Him and the sheep He bought with His own blood. And then— to the altar you go.

Remember to Eat

The French military leader Napoleon Bonaparte is often credited with saying that "an army marches on its stomach."[8] If armies are to fight, they need to eat. The same is true for God's people: in wartime, they need nourishment to fuel their courage. When we look back in history, we see Christians metabolizing Word and Sacrament as they marched in step with our Lord.

God made a solemn promise during Israel's exile: "I, I myself will search for my sheep . . . I will rescue them from all places where they have been scattered . . . and I will feed them on the mountains . . . I will feed them with good pasture" (Ezek. 34:11–14). He made good on that promise, in part through feeding of the multitudes who were like sheep without a shepherd (Mark 6:30–43) at His Last Supper (Matt. 26:17–29), and through giving His body as the bread of life for eternal life (John 6:22–59).

Ancient church leaders understood their ministries to be joining in this work of gathering and feeding God's scattered flock. They accepted that their primary task was to feed their people with "Word and Sacrament." This included Bible and Eucharist, as often as possible, especially in times of danger. These sources of soul nourishment were essential for faithful, courageous warfare. On his slow train to martyrdom, Ignatius encouraged one suffering church to "Come together more frequently to celebrate the eucharist and give glory to God. For when you frequently gather as a congregation, the powers of Satan are destroyed, and his destructive force is vanquished by the harmony of your faith."[9]

When we gather around the presence of Christ, our perspective on our crisis changes. Our souls receive strength and nourishment. We go out ready to engage the crisis with renewed hope and power to transform it. God's Word and Sacrament

> When we gather around the presence of Christ, our souls receive strength and nourishment. We go out ready to engage the crisis with renewed hope and power to transform it.

ministry feeds our people with the presence of Jesus Christ—
His life, death, resurrection, and coming kingdom.

Soon after the persecution subsided in Carthage, Cyprian
returned to a traumatized flock. Betrayed by their own country-
men, these Christians had endured the horrors of torture and
were burying their loved ones. As the plague ripped through
their city, Christians again took the blame from their superstitious neighbors who needed a scapegoat. Would they turn
inward? Despair? Seek revenge? They surely were tempted, as we
would be.

Yet Cyprian knew that this crisis provided a fresh opportunity to embody the gospel. So he gathered as many Carthaginian
Christians as possible in the largest space he could find. Huddled
in a crowded room, Cyprian fed them with the Word of God.
"As he [Cyprian] drew on the texts . . . of the church and applied
these to the people's behavior, Cyprian assumed that the Christians could hear the voice of God. And he believed that if they
genuinely listened to God, the Christians would respond to the
plague in a way that was marked by courage and patience."[10]

Drawing on Jesus' Sermon on the Mount, Cyprian called
them to provide medical care not only for their fellow believers, but also for their suffering neighbors who had betrayed and
blamed them. This was unheard of—hospitals did not exist
before Cyprian's time, and most people were throwing their sick
family members into the streets to bolster their own chances of
survival. Cyprian called his people to stand in the midst of the
crisis, to overcome evil with good, to love their enemies who had
contracted the plague, and to pray for their salvation.

The Holy Spirit moved powerfully among the Carthaginian believers in that meeting, and in the following days, these Christians nursed plague victims, fed the hungry, sat with the traumatized, and prayed for their enemies. Their gospel witness became "most eloquent when they were not in control."[11] The result of this response? Many lives were saved in Carthage, both physically and eternally. Sociologist Rodney Stark estimates the percentage of Christians in Carthage skyrocketed.[12] Their care for the sick beyond their close kin even inspired pagans, who could not deny the power of their sacrificial example.

One of the great challenges for churches is to keep the ministry of the Word and Sacrament going in the midst of crisis.[13] On a human level, we can get swamped, burdened, and reactive. When this happens, we need to lead ourselves to Jesus and be fed by Him. Without Him, we would all scatter on the day of thick clouds and darkness. Yet with Him, we have the nourishment we need, both marching orders and marching bread.

Fight for the Bride

Isn't the bride of Christ beautiful? Yes, she is flawed; that's part of the romance. Her Bridegroom gave His life to rescue her, cleanse her, and present her transfigured in glory forever. Even now, if we look past the scar tissue and lingering blemishes, we can see her glorious beauty. The bride of Christ is made up of women, men, and children from every tribe, tongue, people, and nation. This beautiful, diverse unity came at a great cost (Eph. 2:11–22). And it has great power to sustain our faithful living under fire.

If there was a hill the early church leaders were willing to die on during a crisis, it was the *precious unity of the church over polarization and schism.* They used every means available to fight for Christian unity within small congregations, cities, regions, and even the global church. Like Paul with the Corinthians, this usually took the form of pleading, asking, and encouraging. These early leaders mustered all of their pastoral, rhetorical, and diplomatic skills to keep the bride from fracturing.

For himself, Ignatius sprinkled his letters with metaphors for Christian unity, like strings on a lyre or a harmonious choir. Each diverse member makes a humble, supportive contribution to the whole. "Let there be nothing among you that could divide you, but be unified with the overseer and with those who preside (lead) . . . Let there be one prayer, one petition, one mind, and hope in love and in blameless joy, which is Jesus Christ . . . you should all run together, as into one temple of God, as upon one altar, upon one Jesus Christ, who came forth from one Father and was with the one and redeemed to the one."[14]

Yet when a crisis hits a church, or any group, it tends to become highly anxious. A whole host of divisive activity can result: scapegoating, attacking, gossiping, distancing, and encamping as separate[15] It's worth asking ourselves, "How do I react when I feel stressed or under threat? When I feel anxious, do my behaviors or attitudes contribute to Christian unity or take away from it?"

It's worth returning to the case study of the Carthaginian church in Cyprian's day. On one side stood the "confessors," who had been "imprisoned, flogged, twisted on the rack, starved in dark damp dungeons, and in some cases executed" for their steadfast confession of Jesus.[16] This brought them honor within the community. If we're not careful, suffering has a way of curdling in our hearts. It can purify or it can puff us up. Our trauma makes us untouchable—so we think. The confessors ended up forming themselves into a self-appointed admissions committee. They began to pick and choose who could be readmitted into the fellowship of the church.

On the other side stood the "lapsed," those who capitulated to the new Roman emperor. Some even went voluntarily to the marketplace before they were summoned to offer a pinch of incense to the gods. Others caved in after great duress or threats against their loved ones. Of course, we look upon their dilemma with compassion—their choice was excruciating. The most problematic ones in the bunch, however, were unrepentant. After they sinned with a high hand, they demanded reentry to the church without a trace of remorse.

You can imagine how entrenched these tribes were in their positions. "My body was broken for Christ, and you folded like a coward!" We can hear the confessors lashing out, pain in their voices. The lapsed may have retorted with a condescending eye roll: "Could you calm down please? Love covers a multitude of sins, and the gods aren't real anyway! It's not my fault you don't understand grace." Can you hear the seamless garment of Christ ripping in half?

It takes a wise, less-anxious leader to step in and restore unity in conflicts this deep. Cyprian listened to both sides, resisting the temptation to capitulate to one position or the other. Both had a point; both had a problem. Drawing upon Scripture, Cyprian applied his great pastoral wisdom to stake out a new position: the lapsed could be readmitted to the church, but after a season of active repentance. Confessors should be honored but should cease and desist from their gatekeeping activities.[17]

It's likely that after this decision, both the confessors and the lapsed were equally unhappy with their pastor. I've often heard it said that leadership is disappointing people at a rate they can stand. Yet in the end, Cyprian's unifying work won the day. The patient, slow, and humble work of reconciliation continued, and the garment of Christ was rewoven one strand at a time. This freshly won unity added to the church's courage to bear witness to Christ, care for the sick, and burn brightly as a spiritual beacon in Carthage.

Cyprian's work for unity should not be confused with a pacifying approach that says, "The moderate position is always the one we should adopt," or worse, "The path to unity is helping everyone calm down." Sometimes a moderate position in our eyes is extreme from the perspective of the global church and Christian history. Cyprian shows us that the way to unity is by embracing the authentic gospel, taught in Scripture and lived in the local church. Often the most difficult form of courage is not bravado in the public square but humility

> Often the most difficult form of courage is not bravado in the public square but humility before our brothers and sisters, as we cop to our divisive behavior or errant beliefs.

before our brothers and sisters, as we cop to our divisive behavior or errant beliefs. Only then can we lock arms with the faithful and humbly bear witness with them in the world.

In the end, Cyprian's time came. As persecution flared up yet again in the Roman Empire, he decided the best place to make his final confession was in his hometown of Carthage, before a large crowd including his flock. Galerius Maximus, the proconsul, engaged Cyprian in the following dialogue:

Galerius: "Are you Thascius Ciprianus?"

Bishop Cyprian: "Yes, I am."

Proconsul Galerius Maximus: "Are you the one who has presented himself as the leader of persons holding sacrilegious opinions?"

Cyprian answered: "Yes."

Galerius Maximus: "The most sacred Emperors have commanded you to perform the rite."

Cyprian: "I refuse."

Galerius: "Consider your interests."

Cyprian: "Do as you are bid. In so clear a case there is no need for consideration."

Galerius: "You have long lived in the holding of sacrilegious opinions and have joined yourself very many members of an abominable conspiracy, and have set yourself up as an enemy of the gods of Rome and religious ordinances, nor have the pious and most sacred Emperors Valerian and Gallienus, the Augusti, and Valerian, the most noble Caesar, been able to compel you to the observaction of their rites. And therefore since you have been convicted as the contriver and standard-bearer in most atrocious crimes, you shall be an example to those whom by your wickedness you have joined with you: discipline shall be vindicated in your blood. The pious and most holy Augusti emperors Valerian and Gallienus, and Valerian most noble Caesar, failed to bring you back to the observance of their religious ceremonies.

Therefore, since you have been seen to be the instigator of the worst of crimes, we shall make an example of you before those whom you have associated with yourself in these wicked actions. The respect for the law will be sanctioned by your blood."[18]

Having said this, he read out in a loud voice from a tablet the decree: "I order that Tascius Ciprianus be punished by being beheaded." And Cyprian responded, "Thanks be to God."[19] Right before his death, Cyprian instructed his disciples to give twenty-five gold pieces to his executioner.

I give thanks to God for the example of Cyprian, Ignatius, and the countless other men and women who showed us what faithfulness under fire looks like. May all of us stand in our day when our time comes. As the Queen herself said, we should expect difficulty and not be afraid of it. The Lord is with us, and greater is He that is in us than he that is in the world. Thanks be to God.

ACKNOWLEDGMENTS

Thanks to Drew Dyck and Moody Publishers for their support of this project and partnership in ministry. Thanks to Annette LaPlaca for the edits and direction, Erik Peterson for the beautiful cover, Kaylee Dunn for the graphic design, and to Jackson Ford for the theological research and help with citations.

Thanks to Immanuel Anglican Church for making space for me to write and for the privilege of serving as your pastor. I'm honored to be a fellow pilgrim with you to the heart of God. Thanks to Immanuel's staff for their incredible leadership and support in this process: Nichole, Jennifer, Abigail, Drew, Deacon Susan, and Kayla.

Thanks to Fr. Michael and Liz Flowers for your generous hospitality, daily prayer, and use of your library.

Thanks to my brothers for their ideas, prayer, support and feedback along the way: Matt W., Aubrey, Blake, Dan, Bill G., Trevor, Chad, Josh R., Yosh, Rick, Scott C., Ken, Scott B., Matt R., Josh M., Josh A., Stewart, David W., Jason, Nathan, David S., Travis, Steve, Brian, Nate, Alex, Stephen, and Chris. You guys are the best.

Most of all, thanks to Laura for your love, sacrifices, jokes, and level-headed wisdom, and to August, Samuel, Olivia, and Simona for the ping-pong matches, Harry Potter expertise, and sharing the joy of the journey with me.

NOTES

Chapter 2: Eucharist

1. For a fair and irenic survey of views from Baptist, Reformed, Lutheran, and Roman Catholic theologians, see John H. Armstrong, Paul E. Engle, eds., *Understanding Four Views on the Lord's Supper* (Grand Rapids: Zondervan, 2009).

2. Dr. Boersma mentioned this in a lecture in a reading group on the church fathers in September 2020. For a deeper dive on his perspective, see *Heavenly Participation: The Weaving of a Sacramental Tapestry* (Grand Rapids: Eerdmans, 2011).

3. John Steinbeck, *East of Eden* (New York: Viking Press, 1952), 384–85, emphasis added for clarity.

4. J. R. R. Tolkien, *The Two Towers: Being the Second Part of The Lord of the Rings* (New York: Ballantine Books, 1994), 76.

5. Saint Patrick, *Confession of Saint Patrick* (Portland, OR: Image Publishing, 1998).

6. St. Patrick, in *The Tripartite Life of Patrick* (1887), 315–16, in *Prayers from the Ancient Celtic Church*, collected, translated, and edited by Paul C. Stratman (self-pub., 2018), 29.

7. Michael Reeves, *Delighting in the Trinity* (Downers Grove, IL: InterVarsity Press, 2012), 43.

8. Marcus Johnson and John Clark, *The Incarnation of God: The Mystery of the Gospel as the Foundation for Evangelical Theology* (Wheaton, IL: Crossway Books, 2015), 189.

9. Peter Leithart, *Theopolitan Liturgy* (West Monroe, LA: Theopolis Books, 2019), 109.

10. J. R. R. Tolkien, *The Two Towers*, *The Lord of the Rings*, book 3, chapter 5.

Chapter 3: Baptism

1. Luc Kordas, "The Singular Loneliness of New York City," *Lens Culture*, https://www.lensculture.com/articles/luc-kordas-the-singular-loneliness-of-new-york-city.

2. Ibid.

3. Philip Jenkins, "Is American Christianity Really in Free Fall?" *Anxious Bench*, October 22, 2019, https://www.patheos.com/blogs/anxiousbench/2019/10/is-american-christianity-really-in-free-fall/.

4. Tertullian, *On Baptism*, Ambrose, *Sacraments* 3.3, Gregory of Nyssa, *On the Baptism of Christ*.

5. C. S. Lewis, *The Voyage of the Dawn Treader* (United Kingdom: HarperCollins, 1994), 99–113.

6. Craig Berthnal, *Tolkien's Sacramental Vision: Discerning the Holy in Middle Earth* (Kettering, OH: Angelico Press, 2014), 126.

7. C. S. Lewis, *Mere Christianity* (New York: HarperCollins, 2001), 63–64.

8. Ibid.

9. L. M. Montgomery, *Anne of Green Gables* (New York: Grosset & Dunlap, 1983), 233.

10. Prof. Riley Steffey, "John Calvin on Adoption and Baptism," personal correspondence (2021).

Chapter 4: Time

1. For this and other insights and references included in this chapter, I am indebted to the work and permissions of Rev. Aubrey Spears and his remarkable sermon series An Unhurried Life: Receiving the Gift of Time, preached at Church of the Incarnation, Harrisonburg, Virginia, in September 2012.

2. Dorothy Bass, *Receiving the Day: Christian Practices for Opening the Gift of Time* (San Francisco: Jossey-Bass, 2000), 47–48.

3. Marion J. Hatchett, *Commentary on the American Prayer Book* (New York: HarperCollins, 1995), 134–36.

4. *The Book of Common Prayer* (Huntington Beach, CA: Anglican Liturgy Press, 2019), 71.

5. Ibid., 51.

6. Eugene Peterson, *Working the Angles: The Shape of Pastoral Integrity* (Grand Rapids: Eerdmans, 1987), 68.

7. *The Book of Common Prayer* (2019), 25.

8. Adrielle Pardes, "There Are No Hours or Days in Quarantine," *Wired*, May 8, 2020, https://www.wired.com/story/coronavirus-time-warp-what-day-is-it/, emphasis mine.

9. Abraham Heschel, *The Sabbath* (New York: Farrar, Straus and Giroux, 1951), 3–10.

10. Peter Scazzero, *Emotionally Healthy Spirituality* (Grand Rapids: Zondervan, 2017), 150–63. I appreciate the practical application of the Sabbath laid out in Scazzero's work, applying it to different life callings and situations.

11. Bass, *Receiving the Day*, 13.

12. Paul Bradshaw, *Early Christian Worship: A Basic Introduction to Ideas and Practice* (Collegeville, MN: Liturgical Press, 2000), 75–76.

13. Ibid., 77–79.

14. Eugene Peterson, *Christ Plays in Ten Thousand Places: A Conversation in Spiritual Theology* (Grand Rapids: Eerdmans, 2008), 116–17.

15. Philip H. Pfatteicher, *Journey into the Heart of God: Living the Liturgical Year* (Oxford: Oxford University Press, 2013), 344.

16. *The Book of Common Prayer* (2019), 600.

17. My book *The Good of Giving Up: Discovering the Freedom of Lent* (Chicago: Moody Publishers, 2017) explores this season in more depth and provides practical ways to engage it in a grace-filled way.

18. Pfatteicher, *Journey into the Heart of God*, 173–76.

19. Bass, *Receiving the Day*, 97.

20. Lauren Winner, "Foreword," in Bobby Gross, *Living the Christian Year: Time to Inhabit the Story of God* (Downers Grove, IL: IVP Books, 2009), 15.

Chapter 5: Scripture, Creeds, and Old Prayers

1. Psalm 108, Coverdale Bible Translation.

2. Ibid.

3. Horatio Spafford, "It Is Well with My Soul," 1873, in Robert Morgan, *Then Sings My Soul: 150 of the World's Greatest Hymn Stories* (Nashville, TN: Thomas Nelson Publishers, 2003), 184–185.

4. Remarkably, there was only one copy of this collection of prayers that survived. See "Leonine Sacramentary" from *The Oxford Dictionary of the Christian Church* (Oxford: Oxford University Press, 2005), 976; and Marion J. Hatchett, *Commentary on the American Prayer Book* (San Francisco: HarperOne, 1995), 146.

5. *The Book of Common Prayer* (Huntington Beach, CA: Anglican Liturgy Press, 2019), 63.

6. Justin Martyr, *First Apology*, 65 & 67, as quoted in Frank Senn, *Introduction to Christian Liturgy* (Minneapolis: Fortress Press, 2012), 44–45.

7. Alan Kreider, *The Patient Ferment of the Early Church: The Improbable Rise of Christianity in the Roman Empire* (Grand Rapids: Baker, 2016), 192.

8. Senn, *Introduction to Christian Liturgy*, 44–45.

9. For a deeper dive on this topic, see Normand Bonneau, *The Sunday Lectionary: Ritual Word, Pascal Shape* (Collegeville, MN: Liturgical Press, 1998).

10. Frances Young, *The Making of the Creeds* (London: SCM Press, 1991), 25.

11. Hippolytus, in Alistair C. Stewart, ed., *On the Apostolic Tradition* (Crestwood, NY: St. Vladimir's Seminary Press, 2015), 133–36. I am also indebted to Ben Myers's historic reconstruction of this moment (*The Apostles' Creed*, 1–5).

12. Ibid.

13. Gregory of Nazianzus, *Ep.* 101.32.

14. Hippolytus, *On the Apostolic Tradition*, 133–36.

15. One such example was the Montanist movement. See Young, *Making of the Creeds*, 50–52.

16. Hippolytus, *On the Apostolic Tradition*, 133–36.

17. J. N. D. Kelly, *Early Christian Creeds, 3rd Ed.* (Harlow, Essex: Addison Wesley Longman Limited, 1972), 94–99.

18. Liuwe H. Westra, *The Apostles' Creed: Origin, History, and Some Early Commentaries* (Belgium: Brepols Publishers, 2002), 70–72. Westra takes pains to note that the Apostles' Creed never existed as a pristine document but varied in wording from region to region until Charlamagne decreed otherwise in the ninth century.

19. See his book by the same name.

20. Ben Myers, *The Apostles' Creed: An Introduction* (Bellingham, WA: Lexham Press, 2018), 2.

Chapter 6: Liturgy

1. Fr. Trevor McMacken, "Our Anglican Heritage," City of Light Anglican Church.
2. "The Kenyan Rite: A Eucharistic Service from the Anglican Church of Kenya," Worship Ministries of the Christian Reformed Church, https://www.reformedworship.org/article/march-2018/kenyan-rite.
3. Ibid.
4. *Book of Common Prayer* (2019), 202.
5. Ambrose, *On the Sacraments*, 5:5–7. Note that John Chrysostom warned us from giving Jesus the kiss of Judas by taking part in Communion in an unworthy manner (CCC 1386); see Brant Pitre, *Jesus the Bridegroom: The Greatest Love Story Ever Told* (New York: Random House, 2018), 147–48.
6. William T. Cavanaugh, *Torture and Eucharist: Theology, Politics, and the Body of Christ* (Oxford: Blackwell, 1998), 224.
7. Alan Krieder, *The Patient Ferment of the Early Church* (Grand Rapids: Baker Academic, 2014).
8. Edith Humphrey, *Grand Entrance: Worship on Earth as in Heaven* (Grand Rapids: Brazos Press, 2011), 62.

Chapter 7: Passing the Peace

1. Alan Krieder, *The Patient Ferment of the Early Church* (Grand Rapids: Baker Academic, 2014), 51.
2. Twitter, accessed February 9, 2022, https://twitter.com/maple cocaine/status/1080665226410889217. Hat tip to Samuel D. James, who referenced this tweet in his essay, "Girl, Get Cancelled: Social media, privilege and the social currency of Story," *Insights*, April 22, 2021, https://samueldjames.substack.com/p/girl-get-canceled.

3. Jon Ronson, *So You've Been Publicly Shamed* (New York: Riverhead Books, 2015).

4. Social media is neither "all bad" nor "all good," but a complex mixture. Social media has given a platform for disempowered voices who had been denied justice in other forms. This is especially true for people of color, victims of sexual violence, political prisoners, and many others who have been unfairly silenced. It has also connected people that would otherwise not meet, which has led to healthy collaboration and important dialogue.

5. The exception to this is when kisses were given to a hand or a ring, which signified homage to a higher-ranking person.

6. Paul Bradshaw, *Early Christian Worship: A Basic Introduction to Ideas and Practice*, 2nd ed. (Collegeville, MN: Liturgical Press, 2010), 9–40.

7. Kreider, *The Patient Ferment*, 216–17.

8. Cyprian, *Dom. or.* 23, in Kreider, *Ferment of the Early Church*, 213.

9. *Babette's Feast*, Danish film from 1987 (Santa Monica, CA: MGM Home Entertainment, 2001).

10. Michka Assayas, *Bono: In Conversation with Michka Assayas* (New York: Riverhead Books, 2005), 203–4.

11. If you are interested in learning more about peacemaking, I recommend the following resources: The Emotionally Healthy Relationships course by Pete and Geri Scazzero (emotionally healthy.org), Jim Van Yperen's book *Making Peace: A Guide to Overcoming Church Conflict* (Chicago: Moody Publishers, 2002) and Ken Sande's book *The Peacemaker: A Biblical Guide to Resolving Personal Conflict* (Grand Rapids: Baker, 2004). For abuse prevention and response in the church, check out Victor Vieth, *On This Rock: A Call to Center the Christian Response to Child Abuse on the Life and Words of Jesus* (Eugene, OR: Wipf and Stock, 2018), and Rachel Denhollander, "The Lion and the

Lamb—How the Gospel Informs Our Responses to Abuse"
YouTube video, 50:26, posted by "Valued Conference," April 11,
2019, https://www.youtube.com/watch?v=mQPk5pA0zuo.

12. Songwriters: Michael Card / Niles Borop. "Come to the Table"
lyrics © Mole End Music, Word Music, Llc, Whole Armor
Publishing Co.

13. The historical account supporting this is found in Maureen A.
Tilley, "The Passion of Saints Perpetua and Felicity," in *Religions
of Late Antiquity in Practice,* ed. Richard Valantasis, *Princeton
Readings in Religions* (Princeton: Princeton University Press,
2000), 387–97. I am greatly indebted to Alan Kreider's historical
reconstruction of the events based on Tilley's translation in *The
Patient Ferment,* 44–51.

14. Kreider, *The Patient Ferment,* 48.

15. Fr. Eirik Olsen, Rector of Light of Christ Kenosha, email message.

Chapter 8: The Prayers of the People

1. Scott Eden, "The Burning Desire of Texas A&M," ESPN,
http://www.espn.com/espn/feature/story/_/id/11937545/
texas-bonfire-burns-fifteen-years-collapse-kills-12-students.

2. Rev. John Greenfield, *Power from on High: The Story of the Great
Moravian Revival of 1727* (The Moravian Church in America,
1991), 1–9.

3. Ibid.

4. Ibid.

5. *Didache,* in Bart D. Ehrman, ed., *The Apostolic Fathers,* 14.1–3,
Loeb Classical Library (Cambridge, MA: Harvard University
Press, 2003), emphasis added.

6. Marion J. Hatchett, *Commentary on the American Prayer Book*
(San Francisco: HarperCollins, 1995), 341.

7. *The Book of Common Prayer* (Huntington Beach, CA: Anglican Liturgy Press, 2019), 130.
8. Ibid.
9. I offer some practical training for how to hear and make a confession in *The Good of Giving Up: Discovering the Freedom of Lent* (Chicago: Moody Publishers, 2017), chapter 11.
10. Hatchett, *Commentary*, 163–64. This structure is generally true of most collects, though the features of each collect are varied and multifaceted.
11. Ibid., 598.
12. *Book of Common Prayer* (2019), 598. This is one of Thomas Cranmer's most treasured collects and an example of how poetry and theology belong together.
13. Edwin Friedman, *A Failure of Nerve: Leadership in the Age of the Quick Fix* (New York: Seabury Books, 1999), 51–94. For a practical application to ministry situations, see Steve Cuss, *Managing Leadership Anxiety: Yours and Theirs* (Nashville: Thomas Nelson, 2019) and J. Robert Creech, *Family Systems and Congregational Life: A Map for Ministry* (Grand Rapids: Baker Academic, 2019).
14. Bradshaw, *Early Christian Worship*, 41.
15. Tertullian, *On Prayer* (*De oratione*), 29. Context from Alan Kreider, *The Patient Ferment*, 207–8.
16. Kreider, *The Patient Ferment*, 107.
17. Ibid., 204.
18. *Book of Common Prayer* (2019), 110.
19. Albert Mehrabian, *Nonverbal Communication* (Oxfordshire: Routledge, 2007), 1–15.
20. C. S. Lewis, *The Screwtape Letters* (San Francisco: HarperCollins, 2001), 15–16.

21. Origen, *On Prayer (De oratione)* 31.2, trans. J. J. O'Meara, ACW 19 (1954), 131. As quoted and interpreted by Kreider, *The Patient Ferment*, 205.

22. "Sign of the Cross" in F. L. Cross and E. A. Livingstone, eds., *The Oxford Dictionary of the Christian Church, 3rd ed.* (Oxford: Oxford University Press, 2005), 1510.

23. Tertullian, *The Chaplet or De Corona*, Ch. 3, in Alexander Roberts and James Donaldson, eds., *The Ante-Nicene Fathers: Translations of the Writings of the Fathers Down to A.D. 325*, 10 vols. 1885–1887 (Peabody, MA: Hendrickson, 1996), vol 3, 94–95.

24. Evidence of the larger, expanded sign of the cross appears around the fourth century AD. H. Thurston, SJ, "The Sign of the Cross," *The Month*, 118 (1911), 586–602. Generally speaking, "Western" Christians go from left to right shoulder, and "Eastern" Christians go from right to left.

25. Fr. Stephen Gauthier and Fr. Alex Wilgus, "Incense," *Word and Table*, January 25, 2017, https://wordandtable.simplecast.com/episodes/16.

26. "Incense," Cross and Livingstone, *Oxford Dictionary*, 831. Also "Thurible," 1631.

27. Hatchett, *Commentary*, 152.

28. C. H. Spurgeon, "Golden Vials Full of Odours" (London: Passmore & Alabaster, 1873), 288.

Chapter 9: Mission

1. *Book of Common Prayer* (2019), 137.

2. Lesslie Newbigin, *The Gospel in a Pluralistic Society* (Grand Rapids: Eerdmans, 1989), 116.

3. J. R. R. Tolkien, *The Fellowship of the Ring: Being the First Part of The Lord of the Rings* (New York: Ballantine Books, 1973), 487–88.

4. Craig Bernthal, "The Fellowship Confirmed: Galadriel and Her Gifts," in *Tolkien's Sacramental Vision: Discerning Holy in Middle Earth* (Lechlade, Scotland: Second Spring Books, 2014), 194–214.

5. *The Epistle to Diognetus* (United Kingdom: SPCK, 1908), 63.

6. Rick Richardson, *You Found Me: New Research on How Unchurched Nones, Millennials, and Irreligious Are Surprisingly Open to Christian Faith* (Downers Grove, IL: InterVarsity Press, 2019), 220.

7. *Book of Common Prayer* (New York: Seabury Press, 1979), 107.

8. Dan Fager, "Branch of the Lord," from *Canopy*, released February 10, 2019.

9. Dan Fager, text message, December 8, 2021.

10. I am grateful for my colleague Scott Cunningham for alerting me to this key connection. From "What Is the Church?" sermon preached by Scott at Christ Church Madison, September 26, 2021.

11. Stefan Paas, *Pilgrims and Priests: Christian Mission in a Post-Christian Society* (London: SCM Press, 2019), 190.

12. Deacon Susan Raedeke, "Hoping against Death," sermon preached at Immanuel Anglican Church, Chicago, November 27, 2016.

13. Paul Miller, *A Praying Life: Connecting with God in a Distracting World* (Colorado Springs, CO: NavPress, 2017), 79.

14. *Book of Common Prayer* (2019), 137.

15. Ibid.

Chapter 10: Courage

1. *The National and English Review*, vol. 140, issues 842–844 (1953), 345.

2. C. S. Lewis, *The Screwtape Letters* (San Francisco: HarperCollins, 2001), 161.

3. Pontius the Deacon, "Life and Passion of St. Cyprian" in *The Complete Works of Saint Cyprian of Carthage* (Merchantville, NJ: Evolution Printing, 2013). Robert Louis Wilken, *The First Thousand Years: A Global History of Christianity* (New Haven: Yale University Press, 2014), 67–73.

4. Letters of Ignatius "To the Romans" 4, in Bart D. Ehrman, ed., *The Apostolic Fathers, Vol 1*. Loeb Classical Library (Cambridge, MA: Harvard University Press, 2003), 275.

5. Ibid., Letters of Ignatius "To the Ephesians" 11, 231.

6. Timothy Laniak, *While Shepherds Watch Their Flocks: Forty Daily Reflections on Biblical Leadership* (Charlotte, NC: ShepherdLeader Productions, 2007), 84.

7. Wilken, *First Thousand Years,* 69.

8. Quote Investigator, "An Army Marches on Its Stomach," https://quoteinvestigator.com/2017/10/15/army/.

9. Ignatius, "To the Ephesians" 13, *Apostolic Fathers*, 233.

10. Kreider, *The Patient Ferment*, 66.

11. Ibid., 69.

12. Rodney Stark, *The Rise of Christianity: How the Obscure, Marginal Jesus Movement Became the Dominant Religious Force in the Western World in a Few Centuries* (San Fransisco: HarperCollins, 1997), 73–94.

13. I am not making a statement about how and whether churches should gather, wear masks, or respond to government lockdowns in a pandemic. There are many ways to feed God's people with Word and Sacrament in many different medical emergencies and societal environments. This requires wisdom from above and the grace of the Holy Spirit.

14. Ignatius, "To the Magnesians" 7, in Ehrman, *Apostolic Fathers*, 247–49.

15. R. Robert Creech, *Family Systems and Congregational Life: A Map for Ministry* (Grand Rapids: Baker Academic, 2019), 41.

16. Wilken, *First Thousand Years,* 69.

17. Thascius Caecilius Cyprianus, *The Lapsed: The Unity of the Catholic Church,* trans. Maurice Bévenot (New York: Newman Press, 1957).

18. *Acta Proconsularia, 3-6, Some Authentic Acts of the Early Martrys* (Oxford: Oxford University Press, 1927), 97–98, English translation, slightly modernized.

19. Ibid.

ABOUT THE AUTHOR

Aaron Damiani serves as the lead pastor of Immanuel Anglican Church in Chicago and is the author of *The Good of Giving Up: Discovering the Freedom of Lent* (Moody Publishers, 2017). Aaron writes and speaks regularly about spiritual formation, leadership, and recovering the gifts of the ancient church for today's challenges. His wife, Laura, is a carpenter, and they live with their four kids in Chicago's Irving Park neighborhood.

"Like many evangelicals who love the gospel,
I had my doubts about Lent."

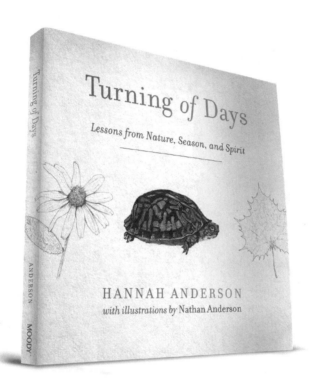

DOES YOUR LIFE EVER FEEL LIKE ONE SERIES OF RUSHED MOMENTS AFTER ANOTHER?

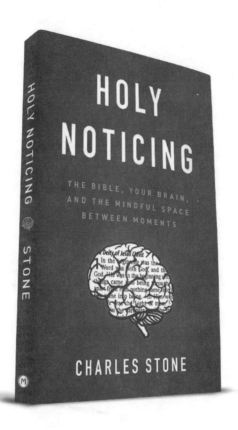